The Changing Primary School

A. B. CLEGG

After his enormously successful influential
book *The Excitement of Writing*, Sir Alec Clegg,
Chief Education Officer for the West Riding of
Yorkshire, England, has compiled a book of equal
importance *The Changing Primary School*. This
new book comprises a collection of statements, all
but two of which are by practising teachers.

The purpose is to give a picture of some of the
changes which have taken place in our primary
schools, of their successes and failures and of the
difficulties which over the years have been
encountered and which in some cases have not
been overcome.

It is a book written in the main by teachers for
teachers and is refreshingly relevant and down to
earth. Most of those who contributed work in
harsh industrial areas where the pupils' homes,
whatever they may offer in care and affection,
give little in educational support.

Some of the teachers who write of their
experiences have taught in buildings the very
existence of which can only be deplored, but they
also know the problems of new housing projects
which in certain circumstances can bear even
more severely on children than do those of more
derelict but more settled communities.

The Changing Primary School will be of
immediate and continuing interest to teachers at
every level who see the educational system
becoming the victim of our rapidly changing
industrial society.

THE CHANGING PRIMARY SCHOOL

THE
CHANGING
PRIMARY SCHOOL

TEACHERS SPEAK ON
ADAPTING TO NEW WAYS

Edited by

Alexander Bradshaw
A. B. CLEGG

SCHOCKEN BOOKS · NEW YORK

Published in U.S.A. in 1972
by Schocken Books Inc.
67 Park Avenue, New York, N.Y. 10016

Library of Congress Catalog Card No. 72–183617

Printed in Great Britain

CONTENTS

Acknowledgements   *page* 6
Introduction   7

1 EIGHTY YEARS OF CHANGE

Eighty years ago   11
Forty years ago   25
Today's school   38
Change: how it came about   49

2 CHANGE AS SEEN BY TEACHERS

A head's view of change   63
A class teacher changes from formal secondary teaching
    to an 'informal' primary school   66
Change as seen by a probationer moving from teaching
    practice to her first teaching post   69
The changing attitudes towards parents   72

3 SOME EXAMPLES OF FINDING OUT

Finding out about shadows   77
The slow learner's writing   80
Mathematical advance   83
Starting to read   85

4 WHAT SORT OF AN AREA DO YOU TEACH IN?

What if your school is in an old run-down urban area?   91
It might be more difficult on a new Coal Board estate   97
The dormitory suburb isn't without its problems   103
What about teaching in a village school?   105
We are in an old building and we have no space   115

CONTENTS

5 SOME PRIMARY SCHOOL PROBLEMS

They must get off to a flying start — 122

Why take them on expeditions? Haven't they enough to
do in school? — 130

Surely with the really slow ones you have to slog at it — 136

What do you really mean by compensatory education? — 141

Deprivation. How it shows and what can be done about it — 155

6 WHAT CAN GO WRONG? — 171

ACKNOWLEDGEMENTS

This book is first and foremost an expression of the wisdom and
experience of West Riding teachers and I would like to thank all
who submitted contributions, whether or not they eventually
found a place in the printed text.

We are all grateful to Mr A. R. Stone whose original statement
'The Story of a School' inspired the book and to Mr W. J. Evans
M.A., formerly Her Majesty's Inspector in the West Riding, who
suggested it should be written.

I must also thank my colleagues for their helpful suggestions
and in particular Miss Rae Milne on whose judgement I have so
very much relied and Mr W. J. Morrell.

Finally my thanks are due to Miss Valerie Garbett and Mr
Colin Wood for all the hard work they have undertaken in
preparing the draft.

INTRODUCTION

The country has just completed its first hundred years of compulsory public education. Our primary schools today are very different from the elementary schools of a hundred years ago because the demands which society makes on them have changed and because teachers' ideas on what children should learn and on how and why they should learn it have changed very considerably.

The purpose of this book is to give a picture of some of the changes which have taken place, of their successes and failures, and of difficulties which over the years have been encountered and which in some instances are not yet overcome.

The series of statements which make up the book have with one or two exceptions been written by primary school teachers whose work has given a notable lead in the areas in which they serve. Most of them work under the severe handicap of teaching in harsh industrial areas where the pupils' homes, whatever they may offer in care and affection, give little in educational support and some of them work in buildings the very existence of which can only be deplored.

The topics about which they have written seldom find a place in books written for rather than by teachers, but their significance is fundamental and they are discussed hour after hour round the bar or in the common rooms when serving teachers who know each other well meet on courses to discuss new ways. How do you manage for space in such an old building? What do you do if you take over a school where the staff are set in their ways? What do you do about discovery methods or R.I. or speech or punishment or mathematics or writing? How do you manage for library books? Which is the more difficult – teaching in a really run-down area or on a new Coal Board estate? What do you do about the very slow ones – or those that are in trouble? What was it really like when you started nearly forty years ago?

That a group of serving teachers have written on these and other topics came about in this way. In 1949 H M Stationery Office, at the instigation of the Ministry of Education, published a pamphlet entitled *The Story of a School*. It was written by Arthur Stone about his experience as a headmaster at Steward Street School in Birmingham from 1939 to 1945. The way Mr Stone taught in those years exemplified some of the ideas of great educationists such as Froebel and Dewey about whom on his own admission Stone knew little or nothing, though he had been excited by Cizek's work and had read the Hadow Report on the Primary School which history may yet decide to be the most significant educational report of the first half of the present century.

In 1947 Mr Stone joined the West Riding staff as a County Council Inspector and in 1969 Her Majesty's Divisional Inspector for Yorkshire suggested that the County that owed much to the ways described in *The Story of a School* might say something of the ways and attitudes it had helped to produce.

Accordingly a meeting of some fifty heads of schools was held, at which it was decided that each should name the topics on which he or she felt best fitted to express a point of view. A considerable number of statements followed, and the most appropriate of these have been collected together in six chapters.

The first of these chapters deals with the nature of the changes which have taken place and the first section of it was written by a man now approaching his 90th birthday. Such vivid personal recollections of what schools were like eighty years ago are increasingly difficult to come by.

INTRODUCTION

The whole of Chapter 1 is a description of eighty years of change. The second chapter deals with change as seen by teachers at different stages in their development. The third presents samples of curricular change. The fourth and fifth deal with the problems which arise from differing social backgrounds and with the non-curricular problems which teachers spend much time discussing when out of their classrooms. The last chapter is a warning of the things that can go wrong if a teacher 'jumps on the band waggon and can't play the instruments'.

1

EIGHTY YEARS OF CHANGE

Eighty years ago
Forty years ago
Today's school
Change: How it came about

Eighty years ago

The following account of his village school of eighty years ago is one of the statements in this book not written by a serving teacher. It was written by Mr William Phillips, a retired industrial chemist and a citizen of the United States, when in his 87th year. He is the son of a Durham miner. His wife many years ago and his elder brother up to the end of the last war, both taught in this country. His son was recently honoured by his country for the distinguished contribution he made to the success of the mission which took the American astronauts to the moon. Mr Phillips's statement was written as a matter of interest for his niece, the editor's wife, and was not intended for publication.

MANY years have passed since I attended my infant school and later moved on to the elementary school. I was born in 1883 in a coal mining village. Most of the men in the village were miners. They were a rough, uneducated, hardworking people. The cottages in which they lived were little better than primitive shelters without sanitation. Outhouses with open middens, one for every two houses, were built in the back street as were the brick sinks, again one for every two houses, which carried away waste water into the sewer below. A single tap in the pantry of each home supplied water. The village was unlighted, and in darkness after sunset. There was no gas or electricity. The Mining Company provided free coal for heating and cooking. Each house had a large kitchen grate and oven. Such houses were rent free, and were considered good enough for miners. Their children, though they might be considered under-privileged, were generally well fed and happy. They liked to go to school, where everything was nicer than at home.

I had to walk almost a mile down a steep hill to reach the infant school as I lived on the outskirts of the village. This was held in a large room or hall, which formed a section of the Wesleyan Chapel. It was not designed to be a school. It was separated from the chapel by a plain brick wall without decoration of any kind except for the varnished wood wains-cotting which covered the lower part. On the wall was a row of iron brackets which held paraffin lamps, but I never saw them lighted. These lamps lead me to believe that the Wesleyan congregation used the school hall in the evenings for lectures or other public events for which the chapel was unsuitable.

The floor of the school hall was filled with rows of 'jump-over' forms with attached desks of a size suitable for young children. A central aisle about 30 inches wide ran between two rows of desks. The ones at the left were for the girls, and the right group for the boys. A shelf was built under each desk. Slots were cut at suitable intervals to hold the scholar's slate. Most of the writing was done on slates, using a slate pencil, which made a very scratchy sound. When it became necessary to clean the writing from the slate, spit and polish was the answer. A good polishing pad was the palm of the hand or the end of a coat sleeve. Slates cleaned this way had a peculiar characteristic odour not entirely agreeable. Sometimes paper and lead pencil were used by the older scholars.

12

There was a gallery built over the main entrance door of the school. A short corridor led from the door and emerged into the school about half-way down the gallery. I used to like to sit in the gallery and observe the activities of the younger children on the floor below. A pleasant noise arose and happiness generally prevailed.

The space under the gallery was used for cloakrooms. To the left – the girls, to the right – the boys. These cloakrooms were partly glazed but were poorly lighted and lacked ventilation. Rows of wooden stands held coat hooks on which to hang clothes. The air was cold, damp and musty. There was no wash basin where children might wash their hands, and no drinking water. The gallery was built to hold five rows of forms and desks.

At the end of the central floor aisle was a big desk and armchair for the schoolmistress, and on each side a blackboard on a movable easel. The easels had holes and pegs so that the height of the board could be adjusted. The rear wall was fitted with cupboards and shelves for storage of school materials.

Because of the steepness of the hill a large cutting had to be excavated to admit the chapel buildings on this site. Part of the space behind the pulpit and choir stalls must have been divided into an office or vestry, toilets and wash rooms, and storage. It is probable that the steam boiler and furnace were located here to provide heat. The school hall may have been heated from this source, but I never saw any steam pipes or radiators in the school. It might be that steam pipes were placed under the floor in trenches. I do remember that the school was very cold in winter, and many of the children including myself suffered from chilblains.

Only the schoolmistress and her teachers were allowed to use the facilities in the chapel. She was called Miss Birkenshaw and she was of middle age and a pleasant disposition. The children liked her. She allowed them plenty of freedom, which worked better than imposing a strict discipline. She got

13

quietness and attention at a word. She never scolded or used corporal punishment. Good order came naturally in her presence. Rarely was there a breach of discipline that deserved punishment but where it occurred the offender had to stand in the corner in full view of the school with a cone shaped 'dunce cap' over his head. It was lofty and reached to the shoulders. The dunce cap was also used on children whose effort was poor. Only once in my final year at infant school did I find myself standing in the corner wearing the dunce cap. This could not have been for poor effort but a lack of interest in the lesson, and possibly an attitude of disrespect for the assistant lady teacher. She was so different from Miss Birkenshaw. Anyhow the lady teacher escorted me to the corner and placed the tall dunce cap on my head. It was quite dark under the cap, nothing could be seen. I, who felt unjustly imprisoned, remedied this by piercing two small holes in the paper opposite the eyes, with a slate pencil. Thus vision was restored. The lady teacher could be seen when she occasionally looked into the corner to see me. Fortunately she could not see the expression of disrespect which had not diminished.

As there were no indoor toilets the children had to be sent out to the playground where the toilets had been placed. At a signal from the loud bell the girls were sent out first. From the main street they had to climb the fifteen brick steps that led into the playground. The girls' toilets were of the most primitive construction and were enclosed in a rough wooden shed. After a certain length of time the signal bell was sounded and the girls returned to school. When the coast was clear the boys were liberated. They rushed up the playground steps to their urinal, which was a long stone trough placed along the wall. No water was provided for flushing this through but there was an outlet at one end which discharged into a ground pipe. A wooden fence hid the trough from view. A favourite trick by some of the boys was to stand on the top step and wet down on the ones ascending. When this happened most of the boys stayed in the street and relieved themselves in the gutter. There was no person or teacher to act as custodian and maintain order and decency in the hilly playground, which had a rough irregular surface, unsuitable for playing games. No organised games were possible.

Again the signal bell would sound for the boys to return to school. This was a great opportunity for rowdyism, which on occasions got out of hand, and Miss Birkenshaw appeared to restore order. Her appearance was all that was required to stop the fights, and the boys returned to their desks at once. At that period children were sent to school at the early age of three and at that age boys had not begun to wear pants or trousers. I remember that I wore a red cotton frock that fastened at the waist and covered the legs to below the knees. On one unlucky day I was returning from school when my red cotton frock came loose and I was unable to fasten it up again. I walked home with bare legs, accompanied by the other children who laughed and jeered at my predicament.

My recollections of infant school are mostly pleasant ones. The children were happy and interested in their tasks, particularly in any form of handwork, such as cutting coloured paper into various shapes – hats, ships and other objects copied from the blackboard. I remember making mats of coloured paper strips, which could be woven into pretty designs. This handwork we were allowed to bring home to show our parents. I liked to go to school and learn things and most of the children were equally happy at their lessons.

The alphabet – A B C's – were learned by frequent repetition of sight and sound of the character. Every child soon learned to sing the A B C song. The blackboard also displayed the letters of the alphabet in both small and capital letters, and these were copied by the scholars on their slates. The characters of figures were learned in a similar way. It became very interesting, when the child was able to count how many fingers and how many hands, or how many of anything. The teens and bigger numbers came later.

The method of teaching how to write was simple and effective. The children practised writing –

Straight strokes –	I l I I
Round O's	o O O O
Gimmy sticks –	⌡ ⌡ ⌡⌡ ⎰⎰⎰⎰ ⌣ ⌣ ⌣ ⌣

The child soon became aware that this was a kind of handwriting which was easily demonstrated on the blackboard. Once he has a knowledge of the alphabet, combined with the ability to write, the child was soon writing simple words, such as – cat and hat. The blackboard could furnish a variety of examples which the children copied on their slates.

The infant school was in no way attached or controlled by the Episcopalian Church, as were many of the village elementary schools. The Minister of the Church never visited the infant school. I can only surmise that the infant school was the responsibility of the Education Committee of the County Council who provided funds for the rental and the salaries of the Headmistress and staff. No religion was taught, no prayers were said, and no hymns sung. It would appear that the young scholars never learned the rudiments of religion unless they were taken by their parents to the family place of worship. I and my brothers attended the Church Sunday School twice every Sunday.

The Wesleyans were a good sized congregation. They supported their own chapel and lay preachers. Their leaders were evangelists. They liked to conduct religious services and often held Revival Services and exorted the people to come forward and be converted to a new life.

When I was about 12 years old and attending the elementary school I went to see one of these revival services out of pure curiosity. As the service progressed it grew more fervent. The visiting revivalist had stirred the congregation to the point where during the singing of a hymn such as 'Come to Jesus while you may', a number of young people would go forward to the penitent form. At the singing of another verse more would follow. I realised that I was standing alone in a pew and they were singing for me. I ran out of the chapel like a scared rabbit.

I do not remember that any inspectors came to the infant school. There were no P.T.A.s, no report cards and no ceremonies of any description. Transfers to elementary school came naturally. I will say that Standard 1 of elementary school added little to my stock of knowledge. I could read and write, draw common objects like pots and jugs, animals such as horses and dogs, birds, hens, trees and flowers, also ships and engines. Some of what I did learn was acquired at home. My eldest brother Tom, who became a school teacher, helped me a lot.

In those days there were no distractions or time-consuming elements, such as T.V. and canned music. Time was spent more usefully. There was time for reading and for recreation.

I estimate that each year about thirty-six children would leave the infant school and move up to elementary school. Hence the total number of children at infant school would be 36 times 5 – 180, but I think this is a high figure.

The village elementary school was built outside the village. It was at least a mile from my home, but above us on the crest of the hill. Children who lived in the village in the valley below had a long uphill walk to school. No transportation was provided. They had to bring their lunch-boxes and tea-cans to school for the midday lunch. There was no dining-room. In winter the fireplace in the large room was surrounded by billy-cans to keep the tea warm.

The school served a number of nearby hamlets, and all the homes north of the railway line. It was a substantial stone building with a slate roof. There were three brick chimneys indicating a fireplace in each of three rooms. It was built in in the shape of a letter L, with the schoolmaster's house built in line. He had a nice home with a garden surrounded by a hawthorn hedge. Out back was a large brick-paved yard with an outhouse, a coal house and a midden in the rear. A door from the yard led into a cloakroom, and from this room another door led directly into the largest classroom of the school. This was very handy for the schoolmaster. His wife brought refreshments to him via this route in mid-morning.

The largest classroom held Standards 4-5, 6-7, 7x. The schoolmaster's desk and armchair were placed left of centre, because of the fireplace in the middle. There were four sections of jump-over desks, all fitted with inkwells. There was room for two more rows of desks, so the floor had plenty of space for blackboards, teachers' desks, and the wheezy old harmonium. In addition to the imposing front door, there were two regular doors, one leading out to the cloakroom and the other to the middle classroom, Standard 3. The far room held Standards 1 and 2. A large door led out of the school yard behind the school. Large windows, with a section that could be opened in warm weather, were placed at regular intervals in the school walls, except in the rear wall of the large classroom where the wall was common with the schoolmaster's house.

The teaching staff at the school consisted of the Headmaster – Mr George Askew, who did 90 per cent of the teaching, two teenage male pupil teachers – my brother Tom was one – a female pupil teacher, and two ex P.T.s of uncertain age. Beck Brown taught Standard 2 and Becky Smiles taught Standard 5. Through all her troubles Becky Smiles tried to maintain a sickly smile, but when aroused by lack of discipline she could box ears and cuff necks in a very determined manner. She carried a small cane, signifying authority, but was not allowed to use it.

Beck Brown had eyes that blinked continually, but were

18

devoid of character. She kept the lesson going in a monotonous way, but made no attempt to maintain attention. If a pupil became troublesome she sent him out to the schoolmaster's desk for a caning. Mr Askew was a hard worker. For one thing, he did several canings every day – three strokes on each hand and a final flogging over the buttocks at the retreat. He pretended to be upset at these events. I never saw a girl punished in this way. The Headmaster's main job was teaching backward classes, which he did with great energy. Sometimes he would get really roused and literally foamed at the mouth. On these occasions the spray was unpleasant. Mr Askew had a liking for Standard 6. This lesson was supposed to end at noon, but often went on ten or fifteen minutes longer, when the schoolmaster hit on an interesting topic. This aroused resentment with some of the boys. One day about ten of them leaped the school yard wall when the whistle blew for classes at one o'clock. For some reason – or none at all – I was in this group of renegades. We ran up the fields for about two miles. Then we decided we had gone far enough. Enthusiasm having vanished, the question of returning to school was discussed and by common consent we returned to school as fast as we could. As we approached the front door the schoolmaster appeared, cane in hand. He had assembled the whole school in the big room. We were a crestfallen crew. He lined us up, and after a few remarks about wicked boys running away from school, who deserved to be punished, he commenced on No. 1 in the line. That was me. I was the most innocent of the group. With his eyes glaring at me he trimmed the end of his cane with a penknife, and ordered me to hold my hands out. He landed the cane hard and it smarted. Then followed a good flogging. Then he proceeded to the next victim. By the time he reached No. 8 he was short-winded – 9 and 10 got off comparatively easily. He ordered us to stay in school at closing-time for more punishment. He kept us waiting while he spent thirty minutes teaching his three pupil teachers.

The lady teacher always broke into tears at these sessions. She was not destined to be a school teacher. She was a very pretty girl, and mercifully a young man married her and took her to Canada to live a happy life. The lesson over, he dismissed the pupil teachers. I should say that it was the schoolmaster's duty to prepare his pupil teachers for the scholarship examination for admittance to a Teachers' Training College. These Colleges were under the auspices of the Church of England and their Principals were usually men of the Church – Canons, Deans, and others. The educational course was two years followed by the Qualifying Examination.

Returning to the renegades, they waited a long time for the schoolmaster to attend to them. This in itself was a real punishment. At last he approached us. He had no cane with him. He looked tired out, and had a sad expression. He sat on the desk-top opposite us and said, 'Boys, I am very sorry that I had to punish you for what you have done. I should not have kept you overtime in class. I will remember never to do it again. I will not punish you again. We will try to forget the whole affair.' Then followed a scene that I shall never forget. The boys arose and waving their hands, cheered the schoolmaster. Without a word he ushered us out of the front door and waved to us as we departed.

There were some pleasant features of the school. The scholars had weekly drills outdoors using dumb bells and wooden staves. The old harmonium was dragged out and Becky Smiles played suitable tunes, such as 'Weel may the keel row' to the banging of the dumb bells and the crashing of the wooden staves as they met in the air. A favourite tune was 'March of the Men of Harlech'. Military style marching was also favoured. On Friday afternoon at three, the whole school was assembled in the big classroom for singing. Songs like 'Ring the bells Watchman, Ring, Ring, Ring' were heartily sung. Becky Smiles had an extensive repertoire. On leaving we always sang 'God save the Queen'.

I do not remember much about the tuition derived in Standards 1, 2, 3. After leaving a relatively placid infant school these classes were pandemonium much of the time. The pupils had much of their own way. This was due to the poor teaching staff. If it had not been for the frequent lessons given by the schoolmaster this class would have been very backward. I remember that I learned to read good books and write fluently, and simple arithmetic gave me no trouble. I enjoyed drawing lessons. Most of my work was done at home encouraged by my brother Tom. It was when I entered Standard 4 that I first ran into trouble. A smart pupil teacher, Stephen Wiseman, was in charge of this class; in fact later on he headed the scholarship list. But that did not help me. The schoolmaster took the class almost daily. He soon discovered me weak in grammar and syntax. He laid me wide open before the class and I had a very unhappy time with him for a few days, so much so that I always forgot what I knew when he threw questions at me. But I soon overcame these troubles. My brother Tom helped me out at home. I read his text books on grammar and syntax so often that I practically memorised the whole subject. I was very good at problems in arithmetic, which was a stumbling-block to most of the pupils.

Another item I remember was the monthly visit of the Truant Officer. I sat nearby and could hear every word that was said. The truant was brought before him. The school-master was present. The Truant Officer proceeded to talk to his victim in a severe and threatening manner, keeping his hands moving in a way suggesting that he was about to seize his prey. This was his method of persuading the child to attend school. But he was as mild as milk and made little impression on the truant. He couldn't scare a mouse.

There was a system of inspection at elementary schools in my days. I understand that this was under the aegis of Government appointed inspectors, who carried out the inspections. On printed cards they arranged a series of problems in various subjects for different standards. At examination time these cards were handed out to the pupils to be solved. The results indicated how well or how poorly the pupils knew their subjects. The results also reflected on the success or failure of the teaching staff of the school. In some way, schoolmasters would get possession of these test cards in advance of the examinations. By exchange of information they could work on the answers along with the scholars to be examined, so they usually passed. I remember working out answers to test cards which usually turned up on examination day. In after years I thought that some of the Inspectors themselves were well aware of these practices. In my school days I do not remember either praises or prizes in connection with these inspections.

In Standard 5 I learned to write a good essay on a book that had been read to the class by Becky Smiles. A book frequently quoted and promoted by the Authorities was *Round the Empire* which glorified British rule and influence in the world.

In addition to school lessons Mr Askew would become enthusiastic about other subjects.

I shall never forget the morning he spoke about the Matabele War, and how the natives by the hundreds attacked our thin red line with their spears, and were mowed down like grass with the newly invented Gatling machine-gun, which fired 600 bullets a minute. Moving his arm in a half-circle and sputtering 'Tuta-Tuta, Tuta-Tuta' as fast as he could, he had the scholars fascinated, and I was sure that I saw natives falling in heaps. It was on such occasions that the class ran overtime. I suppose that in the long run it was good for the Matabeles and the British Empire.

The fine character of George Askew, his generosity and his magnanimity are evident in this story. Here was a man whom one could admire and honour. His grave, bearing a Saxon cross in marble, is in Escomb churchyard. On one panel it is engraved GEORGE ASKEW – SCHOOL-

MASTER OF ESCOMB SCHOOL – and the date of his death. I saw it on my visit to England in 1960 over seventy years after I left Escomb School. I experienced a feeling of pride that I had been associated with such a man, even at the hot end of his cane. I made inquiries in the village but found no one who knew him or his career. Forgotten – and his neglected grave knee-deep in grass and weeds. When I left school he wrote me a testimonial praising my work at school and recommended me to any employer who desired a well-educated and ambitious young man.

In my day Escomb School had no visiting doctor or physician to examine the children. Without doubt some had defective vision or hearing. Except for compulsory vaccination shortly after birth, no preventive medical care was known at school. The children were, however, generally healthy and the closing of school because of an epidemic was unknown, though a common occurrence in the large cities.

Up to Standard 6 the class would number short of forty. Standard 6 would fall to twenty-five. Children who had reached an age over 12 were tired of school; so they quit. I never knew how the educational authorities dealt with this problem. The best thing that could be said of those that dropped out was that they were literate.

In Standard 6 the class read a little Shakespeare, excerpts of which I can recite to this day. At the finish of Standard 6, the school practically disappeared. Two pupils were left who moved up to Standard 7. A short desk stood in a corner opposite Standard 6, and this we occupied. A cupboard with glass doors stood in the same corner, attached to the wall. The first job we were told to do by the schoolmaster was to clean out this museum, dust and repair the exhibits, and put fresh labels on them. One interesting display was a cotton plant covered with bolls of cotton; cotton woven into thread ready for the looms, and samples of cotton cloth in various weaves. There were two stalks of American corn or maize bearing corn cobs, also a corn cob pipe, ground corn,

corn flour and corn oil. There were a number of stuffed birds, including some humming birds, a collection of birds' eggs, and the sword of a sword-fish. There was also a collection of sea shells, and some minerals, including lead and iron ore. When this job was completed Mr Askew put us on algebra which I had started at home from my brother Tom's textbooks. The two of us spent a pleasant time in Standard 7. We received the title of Monitors, fillers of ink wells, sharpeners of pencils, etc. A special assignment of high import was for the two to be sent to the railway depot to collect large bundles of school books, paper and school materials addressed to Escomb School. We took with us two strong poles and rope to enable us to drag the bundles to school. The depot was two miles away, so this was a big job.

But this sort of thing was wasted time as far as my education was concerned. When I began my studies for the pharmacy examinations I realised that all that I learned could easily have been done in the two years I spent in Standard 7. Knowing Mr Askew as I did I am sure that he would gladly have helped me in this study had he known what the future was to bring to me. In fact two years later he was instrumental in recommending to the Durham County Council that I be granted free transport to Darlington Technical College where I could take the studies necessary to become a qualified pharmacist. Mr Askew's older daughter I believe went to a teachers' training college and taught in infant schools. When a new infant school was built alongside Escomb elementary school she was appointed Headmistress. This was some years after I left Escomb. She was of course gone when I visited the village in 1960.

When Mr Phillips left his elementary school his future education was assisted by the Durham County Council in the days of 'whiskey money'. The following paragraph, taken from a later letter, tells something of the rigours which a schoolboy had to face in those days if he wanted to continue his education beyond the age of 14.

I was lucky. I got work in a chemist's shop which compelled me to study the subjects necessary for passing the Pharmaceutical Preliminary Examination. This I did without assistance in my spare moments, mostly after midnight after working a ten hour day in the shop and walking six miles from and to home. This was considered fun seventy years ago. The preliminary examination passed, I found that the Durham County Council would pay my transport to Darlington Technical College where I could attend evening classes in chemistry and other subjects. I journeyed to Darlington a total of thirty-five miles, three nights a week during the four years of my apprenticeship, arriving home home half an hour after midnight after a long walk through unlighted lanes. My mother always had a hot meal ready for me. These were strenuous but happy days acquiring new knowledge. . . .

Forty years ago

'A great demand on memory convicts a subject of being low in educational value'   EDWARD THRING

The writer of this statement has served as an assistant and later as a head teacher, for forty-one years. In the late forties his school was one of the first in the West Riding to adopt new methods, first in art and movement and later in writing and mathematics. He describes the schools he served in before the change was made.

25

As new seams were opened and the big colliery in the village expanded, migrants from other coalfields moved in to fill the 1,000 or more houses which had been built to accommodate them. This estate was known as the Battlefields when, in August 1928, I took up my first appointment in the 400–500 boys' school with a central (selective) department.

My first morning is etched on my memory. The whistle blew and a yard full of noisy, boisterous boys suddenly froze into immobility. A second whistle was the signal for a stampede into long lines, an evolution accompanied by much pushing and shoving. Then, left-right, left-right, class by class into school.

Very soon I was face to face with sixty children sitting in desks in five orderly rows. This first confrontation with, in the Head's opinion, these academic nondescripts was unforgettable. For the most part ill-clad and undernourished, bootless and unkempt, they presented a picture which left little room for satisfaction. Many of them had been running the streets until they were seven or eight as there was insufficient school accommodation available.

The Head was a hard man who imposed harsh discipline. Silence was one of his indispensable conditions. He would not enter assembly until he could hear the tick of the clock on the far wall. 'Prayers' were a disciplinary parade followed by 'Juvenile Court'. At the public canings the victims would often beg to be given 'the rest tomorrow'. He regarded them as savages to be civilised or animals to be tamed, and he left me in no doubt that a commanding presence and a strong right arm were essential.

A book labelled 'Staff Notices' came round frequently and we all had to initial the latest intelligence written therein. Many were notifications of Staff Meetings at the end of afternoon school and during which the Head talked and we listened. More rules were written in the notebook provided for this purpose.

Many of the textbooks in my cupboard never saw the light of day; probably they would have been of some use in a grammar school. Every term, a fortnight was given over to revision and to written examinations, regardless of whether the examinees could read or write. Parents' visits were infrequent but nevertheless exciting as they were made by irate or offended fathers or mothers.

H.M. Inspector saw our weaker brethren and invited them to obtain another post before the next visit. County Council Inspectors' concern seemed to be chiefly with the Time Book or the number of chewed pencils and penholders in evidence. Staff changes were frequent and the Head himself left later to take up a new appointment.

About 1930, on reorganisation, we became a senior boys' school. From the outset the new Head took a keen interest in the life and activities of the village and one of his primary tasks was to acquaint himself with all that occurred in and out of school. The slightest suspicion of anything untoward resulted in an inquiry. He would spend hours questioning and cross-questioning until he discovered the truth. Then in the 'juvenile court', still held immediately after morning prayers, or in cases of more serious offences in a specially called assembly, public confession would be made and the caning that ensued would expiate the misdemeanour.

The Head quickly came to be regarded by the boys as 'all-seeing' and 'all-knowing' and they responded to his awareness. By the end of term if there were any complaints he would send for four or five boys, now termed 'public enemies', and failure to establish their responsibility resulted in their lives becoming a misery until they had found the culprits.

The Head insisted on cleanliness and in these early days ceremoniously carried out frequent 'cleanliness inspections'. 'Get your hair cut' could often be heard. All boots and clogs had to be polished. Some boys had neither and many were fitted with boots supplied by the Lord Mayor of Sheffield's 'Boots for the Bairns' Fund.

The boys gradually realised that the Head was vitally interested in their welfare. A school badge was designed and all were encouraged to wear the school cap. A school song was composed and an elaborate House system was devised and operated. It was the House Master's duty to 'attend' to any boy losing points. The House Shield was awarded at the end of each year.

I was now P. T. instructor in charge of games and swimming. Portable apparatus was supplied. This made a clean break with tradition and provided something new. Many boys, including the less able and 'public enemies', proved excellent gymnasts, footballers and swimmers. The cane never brought tears to their eyes but during a P.T. lesson an order to 'get your shirt on' for some trifling misdemeanour did. The 'dominance-submission' situation softened considerably. I was coming off my pedestal and was enjoying a much closer relationship with the boys.

Woodwork, metalwork, science and gardening came into the time-table. Others on the staff were enjoying the taste of success and exhibitions of work became a regular feature of the school year.

The Head was a great believer in success. Written examinations were given to all (including 'C' forms) and at the end of each term mark lists were compiled. These lists were then packed up and stored away. We were still very much concerned with fault-finding. Every error had to be marked in red ink. At Staff Meetings I drew attention to the fact that in some cases I was writing more than the boys and suggested how my time might be spent more profitably. Invariably 'the Boss' thumped his desk and said, 'You will mark every mistake. You can try your fool ideas when you have your own school!'

But the school became a much livelier and happier place

and some of the work was outstanding at that time. His Majesty's Inspectors and the County Council Inspectors were far more friendly in this atmosphere and had time to ask questions and offer advice in the classroom. Though the situation had changed so much the boys had still to obey instantly, to imitate, to keep still and keep quiet for all formal work. In all subjects they had to do their utmost to beat others and 'be top'. But I had learned that the iron hand did not pay; if boys met with some success, trouble vanished.

In 1936 I was appointed Head of an all-through school in a village of about 450 houses with an approximate population of 1,250, and I had also learned to deal with all administrative and general school organisation.

Though the village was rural in character a fair proportion of fathers were miners. When mother brought her child to be admitted and told me, 'John is four and he's bronchi', or asked, 'Will Miss Wray please change her pants if she wets them?', or when I saw, as I often did, the large fireguard in the infants' room festooned with underwear, I was compelled to see children for the first time without thoughts of subjects on the time-table. This was a well-knit, settled community, and most of the children were related. With very few exceptions, all were well-dressed, well-nourished and beautifully clean. Here was a large family rather than a small army. The Chairman of the Managers, the village policeman, the Vicar and the local chapel dignitaries, were frequent visitors on a social basis. If the 'office' wished to speak to me they rang the shop near the school. This was an atmosphere and environment which contrasted sharply with my previous one.

After a few weeks I suggested that instead of ringing the handbell for 'lines' and marching into the school class by class, the children walk into school as soon as they arrived. We cleared our cupboards of all 'worn' textbooks and had just prepared a huge bonfire when a County Council Inspector walked into the playground. After a word of explanation, he proceeded to select more for burning. When I suggested that our stock of books would be seriously depleted by this operation he said, 'Send in a requisition as soon as you like.' New books, electric lighting which replaced gas lighting, and new furniture gave the school a new look and a fillip.

We were organised in five classes of between twenty-five and thirty children. The time-table was divided into periods of thirty to forty minutes' duration except for the daily ten minutes allotted to speech training immediately after scripture. The children were very friendly and I well remember Sam coming into my room to borrow some books. As I was working with my class I invited him to look in the cupboard for them. Sam said, 'Is them 'em?'. 'Sam Sam' I said, 'after speech training?'. After deep thought he said 'Is them ham?'. In the summer I often heard, 'By, I'm gagged'. 'Get thi-sen a sup then'. (So much for formal speech training.)

The teachers were intelligent and industrious young people. They were alert and very interested. They knew a great deal about their children – their interests and aptitudes and their home circumstances. The children themselves received as much attention as the subject matter to be taught to them. There must have been schemes of work but I have no recollection of them. We had frequent discussions about what we were trying to do with and for the children. The younger children were often taken rambling and knew far more than I did about birds, bees, flowers and trees.

These four years proved invaluable to me. I found that the cane was not an essential piece of equipment; I was now certain that the traditional belief in the efficacy of red ink was a fallacy; that administrative matters were not the main job of a Head. Above all I learned the value of knowing the parents well; of full discussion with colleagues before any development began, and most important of all I learned not to be too hasty in drawing conclusions.

In 1940 I returned to the colliery village as Head of the junior mixed department of the school opened in 1934 alongside the senior school I had left in 1936. The bell rang, the children lined up in the playground and were marched in by their teachers. There was a plentiful supply of textbooks in good condition. The teachers were keen to cover their schemes of work and their aim was technical perfection. Much of the written work was exceptionally neat and tidy. Every room had its House Chart and every teacher a cane. A typical class time-table is shown on page 32.

Knowing the village and many of the parents, now stood me in good stead for the cleanliness and clothing situation had been aggravated because of the war. Coupons were required for soap, shoes and clothing. After a protracted 'Cleanliness Campaign' with Nurse practically living on the premises dealing with verminous heads, scabies and impetigo, I enlisted the help of the NSPCC Inspector to help me to deal with the parents of the children who were still 'offensive'. The Inspector let me know when he could give me a few hours. I would then send the poor youngsters home with a request that mother give them a bath, a change of underclothing and send them back to school as soon as possible. The Inspector would then visit these homes. The result was a stream of mothers 'Don't send the nuisance man will you? I should be so ashamed'. I made use of this opportunity to improve attendance. This lever was successful but there was never room for complacency, and the teachers constantly emphasised the need to be clean and tidy. I am reminded of the teacher, who out of the kindness of her heart, repaired the tears in a boy's jacket and stitched on buttons. After dinner a very displeased mother brought him to school with tears re-opened and buttons missing. 'When his coat needs mending, I'll do it.'

Taking 'Lines' four times a day took a good deal out of the teachers on duty so that they were delighted to finish with them, especially when they found that the children came

	Minutes each week
Registration	25
Religious Inst.	160
Arithmetic	175
English	503
PT & Games	110
Art & Crafts	258
Hist & Geog.	138
Nature Study	66
Singing	90
Creative Activities	—
Recreation	12

9.8	9.35	9.45	10.20	10.40	10.55 / 11.30	12.00	1.30 / 2.20	2.50	3.00 / 3.30	4.00
REGISTRATION	RELIGIOUS INSTRUCTION	SPEECH TRAINING	Arith	Rdg	Eng	Hist	Recit & Literature	Sing	Rdg	Games
			Arith	Rdg	Eng	PT	Needlework	Hist	Sing	Rec & Lit.
			PT	Arith	Eng	Hist	Observation	Geog	Book	Crafts
			Arith	PT	Eng	Geog	Needlework	Obs	Rdg	Sing
			Arith	PT	Eng	Rdg	Art	Art	Rec & Lit	Rdg

in far more quickly without any undue fuss. If a child's misdemeanour warranted it I sent for the parents to make them aware of what was going on and to ask for their co-operation. In many cases concerning stealing, they could tell me that they had been missing money at home 'but he had been blaming one of his mates'. I should think that seventy-five per cent of the children came from homes where angry voices, slappings and hidings, were part of the daily domestic scheme. 'The kids are always under my feet.'

Now that I was beginning to see the whole picture my sympathies were with the children. I made up my mind to work for training in personal hygiene, social training, a natural response from the children, and better teaching.

When I say work, I have to think back to the conditions in which we worked. From 1940 to 45 there were six women each with forty-five to fifty children. For short periods we had seven teachers, which enabled me to form a 'C' class and reduce the other classes to forty-two. Staff absences were more frequent as, in addition to the normal hazards, wives wished to spend some time with husbands on leave or to spend long week-ends with them if they were stationed within travelling distance. Children were often crowded into rooms where there was no direct sunlight for the windows were covered with anti-splinter netting; where long black curtains hung to 'black out' when necessary – a very depress-ing environment now I think about it. For a time we had to spend periods of varying length in the noisome air raid shelters. We all lost a good deal of sleep at night. All this must have added considerably to the normal stresses and strains. Despite all this, we invited parents to join us for our Christmas Concerts and Open Days, to support our Jumble Sales to raise school funds, and to visit if they had any worry about their child.

Schemes of work were very detailed and teachers tried hard to cover them. We had been conditioned by the examination for County Minor Scholarships. After the Composition and Comprehension Tests, Mental Arithmetic, Mechanical Arithmetic and Problems had been marked centrally and the successful candidates notified, a full report was sent in to schools. In 1939 one examiner remarked that 'Very few children used quotation, exclamation, and question marks correctly'. Another, 'It is suggested that simple maps and diagrams form a very useful basis for testing the comprehension of certain types of English passages, and that their use, by enlivening the English lesson, will help to hold the interest and attention of the children'. Arithmetic examiners noted that candidates wrote 'not tort', or 'not toht', or 'Miss Anderson has not shown me how to do these'. We were even asked to enter more children born November to February, whatever their stage of attainment in English and arithmetic. It is not surprising that teachers felt that time spent on other things might be to the detriment of these basic skills and would mean very serious loss to the children when they were older. Therefore, although the time-table gave a sense of mechanical efficiency, arithmetic would sometimes go on all morning so that all would 'be tort'.

In my first few months we discussed our work in these subjects. What could we do to help forty non-readers (twenty-eight to thirty of them in the 'B' class, of our first year)? During singing, teachers 'free' would be responsible for a group of ten children – at most two half-hour periods in the week and almost always working from a *book*. Fifty children did not have a single book at home, ninety-five children had between one and five books, and many of these were of the Christmas Annual type. The Schools' Medical Officer investigated six of their homes for me. Not one book, not one newspaper. In one home, father was suffering from pneumonicoccis and could scarcely speak, mother was working on the land and arrived home exhausted. There was no conversation at all.

After a good deal of correspondence the County Library loaned us 250 books for home reading.

I suggested to the teachers, 'It is better to be over-ambitious than to underestimate one's ability and the intelligence of the children.' At this distance there were many pious hopes!

Teachers were reluctant to take PE or games because of some unkind comments by a PE adviser. However, as a change from being indoors I encouraged teachers to take the children outside for these activities. History, geography and nature study consisted in the main of reading round the class from Piers Plowman, Archer and Thomas, and some set of Nature Readers. The notes were copied from the blackboard or sentences from which one word was missing. In 1941 we discussed how we might present such facts as we considered necessary in such a way as to claim the children's interest and not confuse their memories. I suggested that what mattered was the way the work was treated rather than the subjects of study themselves, and that differences would occur in a progressive way as the children moved up the school. Making models, drawings, maps, charts, or oral reproduction might be better ways of expression than copying from the blackboard. Why not let some children try making their own notes? Written examinations and mark lists could be discontinued.

How could we bring more light and life into our rooms? Art and crafts received little consideration at this time as supplies of stationery and materials were so severely restricted that for some time we had no paint and very little card.

Early in 1943 the teachers handed in their canes to me. We began to have the whole school together for prayers instead of having separate assemblies for the younger and older children.

In 1944 Head Teacher Conferences were called to discuss the teaching of arithmetic, written English and handwriting.

As a result a minimum standard was laid down for *all* children. I did not bring anything of this to the notice of my teachers for I was working to remove the weight from these subjects.

In September school dinners began. The children sat on collapsible forms at collapsible tables, so that occasionally five children disappeared with a clatter as dinners went sliding away. The dinners arrived in containers. There were no washing-up facilities so that all plates and containers had to be washed in the children's wash bowls. Talk was not discouraged and we began to learn far more about parents and relatives, about homes and activities, cinema, dogs, pigeons, pigs, and hens. We saw far more mothers too, 'Can John and Mary go to their Grandma's at 4 o'clock?' 'Can I leave the key with Colin?' Mrs S came, 'Will you ask our Bill to go down to the chemist for me?' I sent for Bill and said, 'Run this errand for your Mum, Bill; you have plenty of time.' A few days later Mrs S arrived again with some similar request. I told her she could see Bill herself. Says she, 'He won't go for me, he'll tell me he'll kick my bloody teeth in.' Bill was as quiet as an old shoe in school.

Towards the end of the war the staffing situation was somewhat fluid. I was now striving to maintain reasonable standards of conduct and work until more settled conditions should prevail. Although all my sympathies were with the children, I caned for disobedience, bad language and impudence, mainly in support of my staff. Thank heaven this did not last long for in November 1945 a first-class man was demobilised and was returned to school. Shortly afterwards I managed to recruit a very good woman teacher. Evacuees had left; direction to the pits was lifted so that many of our 'displaced' children were going to Canada. For the first time our classes were below forty; two hundred and sixty eight children for seven teachers. Stationery and materials were more easily obtainable and we were moving ahead.

EIGHTY YEARS OF CHANGE

I have spent my life as Head of comparatively small schools, so that it has been easier for my door, as with every other door in school, to be literally open. The atmosphere in the staffroom has always been such that all visitors are invited to join the staff for tea during 'break' or for coffee after dinner, since I always join my colleagues at these times. Hence, a 'Staff Notice' has never been sent round.

It has certainly helped me to know all about child/teacher relationships at any given time. It might well be that in making allowances for the impoverished background of many of the children in these years, I did not encourage the teachers to demand enough from them.

In 1946 the Needlework adviser paid us a visit and was so encouraging that this craft took on a new lease of life. In 1947 our new PE adviser visited us and after spending an afternoon with us invited me to go along and see something called 'movement'. I felt then that it was far too informal and airy-fairy. A few months after this an Art adviser visited us. We could not see eye to eye because we could not agree that a child should paint what he sees. But in 1948 I attended a Vacation Course on the Junior School and the developments which followed this seminal course are well known in the West Riding.

The developments referred to by this headmaster were the beginning of a striking revolution in almost every aspect of the work in his school. It began, as he says, with art and craft and movement and almost immediately there came a change in the quality of the writing that was produced. The school became a centre of development. The quality of its work was too marked to be ignored and its headmaster, steeped as he was in the old ways, became a convert. The quality of the work produced in his school and his advocacy of new methods have been a powerful example to other schools over a period of more than twenty years.

Today's school

'The whole matter rests on the best method of awakening
and exercising dormant faculties, of directing and training
them, of giving them material to work on, and finally of
so increasing their vigour, and quickening them into higher
life as to amount to nothing less than a giving practically
of new senses, and creating as it were a new creature.'
EDWARD THRING

IN South Yorkshire there is a small town of 10,000 people
which likes to call itself a village. It is in fact almost
entirely a mining community consisting of two villages, the
old and the new, which was built when the new pit was
opening in 1912 and 'sinkers' and early miners were brought
from Derbyshire and South Wales. The two villages are separated by the main railway line from London to Edinburgh.

The community is served by seven public houses, five
churches, a modern youth club, and an old folks' memorial
centre, now mainly devoted to 'bingo'. Almost all the men
work at the pit but bus loads of their women folk are trans-
ported daily into the wool mills and to a glass bulb factory.

In the twenties the Local Education Authority built five
schools on one campus to serve this community, in addition
to the old wooden infants' school already there, so that there
were eventually two infants' schools, a junior boys', a
junior girls' school, a girls' modern school and a boys'
modern school.

In recent years there have been many changes. First the
junior boys' and girls' schools were amalgamated, then the
secondary schools were amalgamated; the infants' schools
were rehoused in new buildings, the secondary schools were
replaced by a large comprehensive school on another site
and the the juniors who were left were organised into two
mixed schools and spread through the old campus buildings.

The school inherited an interesting tradition. In the early

fifties a new Head had developed what was in those years a very new approach. Examinations and streaming were abolished. 'Movement' as it came to be called, became dominant in the school followed by art and good expressive English. At that time the school came in for a certain amount of derisive criticism which was, however, soon silenced by the quality of its work.

In 1962 there was another change of Head and in 1965 the school moved into the secondary school building, which was a single storey building arranged around a central lawn planted with trees and forming the living space for silver pheasants. Circulation in the school was by means of a corridor running round this quadrangle.

By any standards, this school, in which over eighty per cent of the pupils are miners' children, is a good one. For many years no child has been 'referred' for special educational treatment, no child has appeared before the juvenile courts and it is rare indeed at the end of the year to find any child who has not at least made a start with his reading.

Such is the reputation of the school that a number of the county's advisory staff decided to visit it and to describe what they found.

They arrived one day at 8.40 a.m. The school, which opened officially at 9 a.m. was already full of children and staff, despite a dense fog. Many had already settled to work in the classrooms and in the corridors which were obviously used a great deal as extensions to the classrooms as they were full of books, plants, paintings and a whole variety of displays.

The visitors made their way to the Head's room which they found attractive and relaxing and a mirror of the order that was typical of the school. Here they were told that the school was organised in fourteen unstreamed classes, some of them with children of differing ages. There were fourteen members of staff, half of them twenty-five or under, four between twenty-five and thirty, and the remaining three over thirty. Three of the staff were graduates, and three had trained to teach as mature students, one of them having first joined the Merchant Navy and later spent eight years at the coal face.

LOOKING AT THE CLASSROOMS

In the first room, cupboards were arranged at right angles to the walls forming bays for reading in which were lengths of well-worn carpet on which children could sit. The bays were also used for music, writing and for washing-up as the room fortunately possessed a sink.

Fabrics which covered the back of the cupboards served as a background against which were displayed objects likely to interest the children – collections of tree barks, an old apothecary's balance, some mathematical instruments, a display of grasses and dried stems of hogweed.

The second room used to be a science laboratory in the old modern school days. It was a large room with benches round the sides which had been cut down to junior size. It was also fitted with sinks. One corner of the room was devoted to mathematics and contained mathematics books and equipment. Another section of the room was being devoted to a study of water and a diagram showed the domestic water system of a house. Also on display was a glass case containing two stuffed seagulls and a herring gull and two large pictures by children of the seagulls and of a weasel attacking a rabbit.

Along the back of the room was a large fabric and embroidery picture of a Viking and a most attractive nature display and a large landscape picture. In the centre of the room was yet another display of gnarled and knotted pieces of wood, old tree roots, bark, fir cones, animal skulls and a jaw bone with reference books open at the appropriate pages. This particular display was backed by a beautiful piece of tie and dye material.

There was no teacher's desk in the room.

The third room was also large and had been divided into varied and interesting spaces by the arrangement of furniture. In the old secondary school it had been a housecraft room and therefore had a good store room and a sink. It too had its displays, some emphasising textures, some coloured glass and one showing materials from other countries which had been borrowed from the School Museum Service. There were also in this room displays of the children's own work, both their painting and writing.

LOOKING AT THE CHILDREN

In the first room some children were painting and making leaf prints, some were drawing with pen and Indian ink, others were reading and writing or working in clay on the narrow tables arranged in the corridor. There seemed to be no time-wasting and one felt that the teacher, a probationer of four weeks' experience, had very sensibly avoided the pitfall of providing a greater range of choice than he himself could organise. But there was a greater variety of choice than appeared at first glance; the leaf printers were using three different media and their interest had spread to rubbings of wire netting, brick textures and grained wood, and this was obviously capable of further development. Painting brushes and drawing paper varied considerably in size as some pictures were destined to illustrate topic books.

In the second room groups of children were scattered about the room working and there was a quiet hum, disturbed occasionally by the banging of a hammer. Two boys were chiselling away at an old piece of oak which was originally an old school desk top. Three others were working on a boat. Two girls were also chiselling and filing an old desk top to produce a relief picture of a medieval knight – the ringed mail being cleverly shown by curving cuts. Five boys were intently sketching birds in pencil and beside them two others were making pen and ink drawings of a knotted old piece of wood. Four girls were at easels painting bonfire night, the sea and a witch. Beside them two others were painting on a large piece of paper a harbour scene, each house being painted with great care and detail. Two girls were doing multiplication sums with an abacus and one worked so quickly that the visitor had to ask her to do it slowly so that he could follow. 'Yes,' she said, 'I chose to do arithmetic rather than paint. I like arithmetic, I am not good at painting.' She was making up her own sums which calls for more initiative and mathematical understanding than working from the page of a book. A group of girls were working on very large pieces of hessian, making pictures with materials and embroidery cottons. More children were working at mathematics and one girl with an abacus was having difficulty. The boy next to her smiled and said, 'That's not right,' and helped her to use it correctly. One boy working on a fabric and embroidery picture of a dinosaur in the mountains stopped and went over to help his friend who was having difficulty with his pencil sketch of a hovercraft which he wanted for the water project.

In the third room the teacher was a young married woman with little over three years' experience. She encouraged her pupils to choose a medium in which they could work and the children responded confidently and purposefully. They produced some particularly interesting needlework pictures, the older children were the more skilled, no doubt because of their maturity and because of the work they had done the previous year; the younger ones were still learning to make some of the stitches they would require.

Later in the day after a 'movement' session in the hall these children turned to their writing books making up their own stories.

A number of the children in this seven to nine age range wrote with considerable fluency of expression to which both the work they were doing and the written work on the walls bore testimony. Because of the age and ability range of the group there was naturally a great variety of achievement, but the work of all the children was accepted for the effort and endeavour it represented and the teacher gave appropriate encouragement. Some of the children went on to arithmetic, and two girls spent a considerable time collecting from their colleagues information on which they intended to make a graph. They worked in the corridor through the lunch-hour preparing this material but longer time than the visitors could spare would have been required to grasp its full significance, and draw conclusions from it.

... THEIR ATTITUDES AND BEHAVIOUR

The visitor to the first room reported that the children welcomed her and accepted her as one of the group. She wrote;

'One commented that it wasn't a very nice day and got on with his pen and ink drawing. I sat in the writing corner which seemed appropriate as I was scribbling, and my neighbour waited for a convenient pause in my hasty note-making to thrust a word book at me and say 'Is that "Hairy"?' When he too had reached a pause I discovered this was Neil who was making a book on large and small animals. He was obviously a close friend of Mark who found reading and writing difficult but I suspect stuck at it in order to work with Neil. The two were not far apart all morning. When Mark had gone off to the book corner (to consult a picture I suspect rather than the text) Neil said confidentially, 'You know the boy next to me. He doesn't know how to spell "eggs".'

'Roy and Peter who had reached a suitable stopping place in their work decided to have their milk and helped themselves from a table nearby. While drinking they invited me to look at the class books made a week or two previously – on the Finningley air display and on trees and birds. Mark and Neil could be overheard discussing the spelling of "breasts". Mark was obviously much respected for his ability to draw aeroplanes. The teacher asked quietly from across the room if Mark had borrowed his rubber. Despite the activity in the room and his inexperience, there was no need for him to raise his voice. I thought of my own early days of teaching when the whole class would have been stopped possibly with a clap of the hands to discover the culprit who had the teacher's rubber. Mr U had been interrupted in his moving about the class from group to group by a request for dinner numbers. He quietly asked Darrell to go into the quiet room where he knew Royce was working to ask him if he would be staying for dinner. Later Royce told me he liked working in the quiet room, which incidentally had recently been provided with a full-sized carpet and underlay by two of the parents – a Christmas present for the headmaster.'

LOOKING INTO THE HALL

One visitor observed that there was no apparent break between the early activities and the mid-morning assembly.

This he said was particularly noticeable when it came to clearing up. There was no apparent break between activity and clearing up, no loud announcement. The children quietly cleared away, they were used to doing it, trained to do it, and made no fuss or bother about it. When they finished they opened a reading book or started some writing without being told, and carried on until everybody was ready for assembly.

Another visitor later commented on the way in which the children walked quietly into the hall for assembly and sat down with their friends where they liked, to a recording of some Indian music which seemed to appeal more to them than to her. This assembly was for the third and fourth year children and consisted of a hymn sung extremely well and a prayer. The children returned to the classroom by themselves and as their teacher had been taking assembly they, without being told, took out some work and carried on until he returned.

With fourteen classes the use of the two halls necessitated a more predictive programme than one would ideally wish. One class was very soon ready for its turn for 'movement'. The hall had a sprung wooden floor, and the children were barefooted, the boys being stripped to the waist. The children worked intently, the silence being broken only by heavy breathing and the thud of feet. They were obviously thinking carefully about what they were doing – a handspring was followed by a forward roll on the bare boards, or a hand-stand was followed by a roll forward and then backward roll. These sequences are worked out by the children themselves and a considerable degree of control was obviously needed in order to do rolls on a hard wooden floor. The lesson was mainly concerned with contrasting quick and slow movements and finally the children work in pairs.

After changing in the classroom they had only time for a few minutes' reading and returned to the hall for an early lunch, as three sittings are necessary for school dinners. They sat in tables of eight and served themselves without any fuss. Conversation was carried on throughout the meal. The Headmaster considers the reduction of noise and bustle achieved by smaller numbers at one sitting amply justifies this and also provides a long lunch break for voluntary clubs in which teachers and children participate with enthusiasm.

During the lunch-hour the children were free to work in the classroom or to visit the HORSA hut where they could play table tennis or snooker on a miniature table. In this room were also games such as darts, draughts, dominoes and 'scrabble'.

The animal enclosure also attracted children. In it there were ducks, geese, guinea fowl, bantams, fantails, doves, rabbits, hamsters and guinea pigs. Some children fed the animals, some cleaned them out, while others watered the plants in the greenhouse. There was football in the field and games of chess surrounded by interested spectators in the 'chess room'.

The school seemed to be freely open to visits by parents. A large number of adults attended one assembly and one was carrying a baby. As she entered the hall Darrell looking at least two inches taller took charge of her and with a younger child sat as close to her as possible, his earlier dissatisfaction with his pen and ink sketch forgotten. His younger brother, a seven-year-old, was, after three weeks, still feeling insecure in his new surroundings and his mother called into school and stayed with him when she could spare the time. After assembly, Royce's mother spoke appreciatively of being allowed to come into school and then went off 'to help with the tea'.

Another visitor made a similar observation.

'The two brothers Charles and Bobbie, who both had speech difficulties as well as finding it difficult to become part of the group, had their mother in school. Bobbie very rarely moved away from his seat preferring the security of being near his mother. She felt that by coming to school, working in the classroom with her children had helped them a great deal, and she herself had been helped to understand their problems much better.

Frequently other children's mothers came to work in the classroom and the class teacher felt that the help they gave, particularly in hearing children read, and providing this kind of security for their own children, was invaluable.'

There were also other visitors to the school that day. The new comprehensive school was on holiday and a number of former pupils came back to their old school. One of the visitors reported an interesting conversation with two who were in their first term in the secondary school:

'Do you like it up there?'

'Yes. It's smashing – you can do more things.'

'What sort of things?'

'In the gym – there's a gym club, athletics and all things like that.'

'I expect you found it a bit strange at first.'

'We were always changing. You'd just get started and have to move to another room and at first you'd go up the wrong staircase and couldn't find the room at all. Now Mrs Atkinson who takes us for local studies – she stays with us all Tuesday afternoons and all Wednesday mornings as well and you can get something done.'

Keith – 'Do you know the Headmaster?' – 'Yes.'

'He's all right. He's a nice man. He doesn't shout at you. If you do anything wrong he walks over and tells you off quietly. He's nice.'

This lack of shouting and hitting was commented on frequently by the older children and I asked why they expected to be hit. They agreed they were never touched in the junior school. The boys sometimes get a clip for swearing at the dinner ladies (which they thought fair enough) but 'the girls never get touched'.

They told me they missed painting and music. 'You only get a double every week – and you don't get a right lot done.'

Meanwhile a party of eighteen students from a nearby College of Education arrived to bring yet further material to interest the children. They scattered round the school to work in six groups of three. Some were to take children on expeditions, others to work with them in the quad or other parts of the school. It seemed a harmonious and mutually beneficial arrangement – the future teachers learning about children in a natural situation likely to build up their confidence and the children enjoying the luxury of additional adults prepared to be interested listeners from whom they could learn.

The school was now charged up for the afternoon. There

47

was no sharp division in the programme but mathematical situations appeared to be more in evidence.

The school has a concerned staff, as a few quotations from the visitors' descriptions will show.

'Back in the classroom the young teacher was concerned about giving enough time to some of the group (including Mark) who still needed reading practice and had limited the range of choice. Most were getting on with their topic books, some were reading simply for enjoyment. The morning ended with a song to the teacher's guitar and the children went off to dinner.'

'The teacher moved about the room helping to pull out a stubborn nail, asking questions of one child, encouraging another, allowing the children to talk and discuss as they worked and yet somehow he managed to keep the noise down to a quiet hum of activity: organising, helping, encouraging, teaching without apparent effort or fuss.'

'The young teacher was obviously worried about organisation, something he would learn with experience. In four weeks he had established a delightful contact with his class and was learning rapidly to teach in this much more subtle way, asking questions, giving specific help when it was needed, providing appropriate materials – teaching far better than I did as a beginner.'

'After doing his mathematics obligingly, Royce returned to his main interest in the silver pheasants with which he started the day. Lying on his stomach on the quad lawn he was drawing these stately black and white creatures with their scarlet legs. He looked with absorption at one only a few feet away and one could sense an understanding between them. As the Head and I approached quietly this spell was broken and the pheasant uttered a warning call. The child looked startled and the Head said quietly, 'Stay where you are, Royce. He never attacks children and we are leaving you.' As we retreated the bird and the child again seemed to understand one another.'

'A place in which children can live a full day' was the Headmaster's description of his aim for the school.

Change: How it came about

From the three previous statements it is clear that the changes which have occurred in our education service over the last 100 years have been very great indeed.

Some of these changes are easy to describe and to explain. We know for instance how payment by results came about and why it was stopped: we know why at a later date people started thinking of selection and why they now want to end it. We know that at the present time we are doing a great deal for the brightest and for the least bright of our pupils but not enough for the less bright. And of course we know a good deal about curricular changes; there were those capes and bays and dates of Kings, the moral songs ('All I drink is water bright'), the object lessons and the compulsive force which made us always begin with the Ancient Britons; and there were the dumb-bells and those yards of parsing.

But how does change come about? The purpose of this chapter is to state briefly how the changes in primary education which have covered the country in the last fifteen years came about in one large county. One teacher described how she taught before she felt the influence of the change and how she taught after she had been affected by it.

IN the late forties there were many teachers who had come back from the war to find the schools of the West Riding working very much as they had worked in the late thirties. But there were people working amongst the schools who were anxious to see change. The Art adviser in the County had worked with Cizek, one of the PE advisers was an eminent disciple and friend of Rudolf Laban, a newly appointed County Council Inspector had recently written *The Story of a School*, a pamphlet sponsored by the Ministry of Education and published by HMSO in 1949.

In the summer of 1948 the Bingley Vacation Course had gathered together a hundred or so teachers who wanted to be told 'how to do it'. They were not so told. They were required to 'do it' themselves. They painted, they 'moved' and they wrote at their own level of experience, and they were somewhat derisive and even ribald about what they were required to do.

The course was probably less than five per cent successful. But in two or three schools, not more, the seed was sown. Children's painting, the like of which we had not seen before in the area came from two schools which served the mining communities at Thurnscoe and South Kirkby. Then came the following minute from one of the assistant PE advisers:

'The progress of this school and the new approach is steady. The art side still leads, and flowers more fully each term. I think that the art is really the best I have ever seen or imagined from a junior school but the result of the whole philosophy in practice is that this interest and learning process so evident in the art is beginning to affect the academic side. But there are difficulties. The development of the art rests upon sufficient paper and art materials, and since every child is pouring out its ideas boldly and increasingly, naturally there is a much greater demand. In addition, on wet days in the dinner-hour there have been as many as 180 children found in the classrooms working unsupervised, seriously and fully absorbed in painting, modelling, writing and reading. This has necessitated having the materials available for them. It is to be noted that there is no waste of materials owing to the children's control, but there is a problem of composition books. Whereas a child used to take eighteen months to fill a book they now in some cases use as many as a book and a half a term. I am sending you some evidence of this with notes so that you will see what I mean. The awakened imagination and freed expression is beginning to produce a flow of language that cannot be stopped, and the requisition for exercise books and other materials is becoming a problem'.

In the Castleford area there developed in one school a form of 'expressive movement' and we were worried in those days because we did not know whether this was PE or drama and for some obscure reason we thought it important that we should.

Those of us who were administering the service at the time and observing the schools suddenly saw the obvious, which was that all these expressive activities in art, drama, movement, and later in writing, had the same aim; children were being led into experiences which stimulated their powers of expression. The growth of the child as a personality was becoming more important than the teaching of separate examinable subjects, and gradually it came about that every child mattered. Within a few years there were not two schools out of a thousand working in this way, but a score or more, and today it is hard to find a school that is not influenced in some way or another by the new ways. And from these developments we have learned much.

One teacher who was aware of the way this change affected her has written of it in these words:

THE CHANGING PRIMARY SCHOOL

Nearly twenty years ago I taught in a five-class junior school in a small North Yorkshire market-town.

As a young teacher I was willing, energetic and conscientious, but, as I realise now, somewhat unenlightened, unquestioning and quite content to find myself part of a solid framework of routine and conformity.

My classroom was small and dusty. My desk was very high and narrow, and facing me were rows of iron-framed desks placed close together. I knew little or nothing about the children in my care, other than their faces and scholastic abilities presented to me each day.

I worked hard and prepared my lessons carefully. Each evening I diligently marked – in red ink – the work the class had done that day. I often painted large pictures to illustrate my lessons in geography, history or nature study. These pictures were displayed on the classroom walls, along with carefully lettered charts of arithmetical tables, lists of words I considered may be useful, an elaborate Star Card, one or two commercial pictures and about half a dozen of the best paintings or drawings done by the children in the last weekly art lesson. These, of necessity, were always about the same size – all small – because the dual desks afforded little space per child – and all thirty-six children painted or drew at the same time – on Tuesday afternoons.

Every morning at 9.0 a.m. we assembled for morning prayer in a large room that served as hall and headmaster's classroom. The children shuffled and nudged each other as they stood in crowded rows facing the Headmaster. It was rather a rushed service in which we sang a hymn from well-thumbed hymnbooks. There was no atmosphere of worship, no feeling of reverence, no music, no flowers. The prayers were phrased in archaic, unfamiliar language and were therefore incomprehensible to the majority of the children.

We dispersed quickly to our classrooms and each class

had a twenty-minute scripture lesson. I told my children stories from the Bible and the class listened avidly, accepting Noah, Joseph, King Ahab and St Paul as eagerly as they accepted Winnie the Pooh, Tom Sawyer, Sir Lancelot or Peter Pan. I do not think it occurred to me to attempt to relate the teachings and meanings of the Bible to the daily lives of the children in this quiet country town.

After scripture we had arithmetic, and this was considered a very important hour of the day. The lesson began with everyone chanting tables – multiplication, length, weight, capacity and time. We counted in twos, threes, fives, tens and twelves. I asked many quick-fire mental arithmetic questions, and frequently each child had then to write the answers to about twenty further questions. I jotted the scores down in my notebook, thinking that these bits of information would be useful at term end when I wrote out the reports for parents.

A star was awarded to each child who had twenty correct answers. I did not realise that the brightest children did not need a test – except for adding to their glittering row of stars – they knew the answers already and did not need the constant repetition. The less able children did not need a test either, as quite obviously, they had not understood all this talk about gills, hundredweights, furlongs or leap-years.

We had textbooks, and, after the mental arithmetic, all the children would receive their exercise books. Each page would be creased downwards, then two margins would be ruled and all would write the date. The class would work from the textbooks – doing several mechanical sums, and, if time allowed, they would go on to the problems. (Some children hardly ever had time for the latter!) The clever children would speed along, and the not so clever would drop further and further behind, getting more and more disconsolate.

The artificial barriers caused by the names 'Mental', 'Mechanical' and 'Problems' show clearly the attitude we had towards the teaching of mathematics in those days. The children spent years grinding away at mechanical sums and being drilled by rote with little or no understanding. In fact they were 'playing with the tools without ever doing the job.'

During the scripture and arithmetic lessons the children were seated at their desks continuously. I do not think we teachers appreciated the abnormality of confining lively youngsters to this cramped position for so long.

Every Wednesday we had a composition lesson. I selected a subject, and after the children and I had fully discussed it, and many useful words had been written on the blackboard, the children began to write in their lined exercise books. I positioned myself by the easel, ready to write on the board any word that was required. The subject probably did not interest many of the children, though I tried to be original and think of varied topics. The result of all this was that during the evening I marked thirty-six pieces of almost identical writing. The discussion, and the words on the blackboard, had conditioned every child and put them all on the same train of thought – so any imaginative child who had an original idea, conformed to the general, and unconsciously allowed his spark of originality to be submerged.

On Mondays I gave the children ten words to learn, and every Friday we had a spelling test. These words, from a little book of spelling tests, were quite unrelated to each other, or to anything we had experienced as a class. The same children, week after week, were awarded a star for an all-correct paper, and the same children, week after week, struggled to acquire one or two red ticks.

On Tuesdays and Thursdays we did English exercises out of a textbook. These exercises consisted of ten short sentences that had to be punctuated or completed; changed from singular to plural; changed from masculine to feminine or changed from direct to indirect speech. Verbs, nouns and adjectives were all juggled with, as were adverbs and prepositions.

We had comprehension tests, and quite often we spent a half-hour on dictation. Great importance was given to identical layout of for example, the margins and the date; when working from a printed book the page number and exercise number had to be written in a particular place on the page, and then carefully underlined.

It never occurred to me that these children, given the opportunity and encouragement to write freely, were very capable of expressing their own feelings and ideas – but we never gave them a chance! All was directed and imposed.

For PT we took the children into the playground. Jackets and pullovers were left indoors and exchanged for team-bands. The PT was based mainly on the 1933 Syllabus, with leg, arm, trunk and balance exercises prescribed by the teacher, but the emphasis was on team work and quick responses to the teacher's directions and whistle blasts!

Geography, history and nature study lessons were all taken from sets of printed books. The children were occupied in copying such things as sketch maps, costumed figures and seed dispersal diagrams into their exercise books – all with appropriate notes. I spent much time and energy on making Time Charts, mounting illustrations from various monthly educational journals and painting or drawing in ink maps, diagrams and pictures.

I was responsible for the needlework done by girls in the first and second years, and the girls in the Remedial Class. I had these fifty girls, altogether, in one room every week. (The boys went elsewhere and were taught such things as how to bind books, how to make a cane-work rim round a teapot stand, and how to make a book-mark.) After the girls had sewn mats and kettle-holders, I showed them how to cut out and make themselves an apron. The girls chose the colour of the gingham – they could have red, blue or green check. They decorated the aprons with rick-rack braid and the pockets sported a motif.

The outside world lay beyond the classroom walls, yet no one ever ventured there. The red brick building with high windows and a high wall surrounding the tarmac playground where boys and girls played separately was our world, and what was beyond did not exist for us during school time.

It was a safe, secure and unchallenging world. All was prescribed and orderly, and rather dull. But we were a kindly and interested staff and the Headmaster used the cane only very rarely.

Every week was like the one preceding it and we knew with certainty that next week would be the same, and it seemed quite natural to accept this without question.

AFTER THE CHANGE

The school in which I now teach is a suburban infant school. The day begins with a wide range of activities. The children settle quickly to their own choice – it may be painting, modelling in clay or with waste materials, drawing, fabric work, writing their own thoughts on some topic, reading, building, baking, imaginative play, woodwork, play in sand, water or clay, or music making. An engrossed child will continue over a long period – seven-year-old Jane spent eight hours on a small painting using a fine brush and thick paint she mixed herself; six-year-old David spent three days writing continuously about the coal mine, and six-year-old Karen made a thick book all about her holiday in Germany. Many times there is the plea at lunch-time, 'Can I stay in and finish it?' I remember the loud noise of the fixed seats being banged upwards and the excited surge towards the door as the children eagerly poured out of the classroom in my earlier days.

What now of the mats, kettle-holders and gingham aprons? The boys and girls can choose to sew whatever they wish. The fabric box is bulging with inviting colours and textures from satin and organdie to tweed and fur-fabric. I am amazed by the dextrous use of scissors, thread and needles, the bold and colourful collage and the delicate thread-like fabric pictures of flowers or grasses. They do striking, uninhibited *appliqué* work depicting scenes or ideas as varied as The Nativity or impressions of the local wood yard. These infants are also competent doll makers and doll dressers, puppet and soft toy makers. They knit themselves slippers, scarves or bonnets, and can make themselves simple garments – even a gingham apron – if they wish!

These varied activities are followed by a few quiet minutes of discussion and talk. The day of the unrelieved diet of Bible stories has gone. Today with emphasis on the main Christian festivals, we use stories from the Bible or the life of some great person or even contemporary news to illustrate a moral point. Our daily assembly is a short but simple and reverent service.

When I came to this school I was determined that the children were not going to leave my care without some good understanding of basic number concepts. For these children, the days of arithmetical drill, and little skills, mechanically performed, were over.

The tradition that one must get the children to 'do sums' as soon as possible, dies hard. It has, in the past, been quite difficult to convince oneself, and the staff, that an interesting mathematical experience, quite possibly without any recording at all, is far more valuable than a page of neat little sums done mechanically by rote.

I ordered ladders (miniature size), pegs and peg boards, liquid measures, vast collections of well-made toy animals, cars, aeroplanes, and boats; collections of small everyday objects, polished wooden sticks, yards and yards of clear adhesive for covering the assignment cards, plenty of clear plastic boxes for storage, yard sticks, trundle wheels, tape measures, clock faces, clock tracers, clock stamps and stamp pads, polished wooden cubes, wooden beads, scales, balances, water trolleys, sand tables, baking utensils, clothes pegs and interlocking bricks.

We set to work and devised how best to use these colourful and exciting materials. The work was carefully thought out and graded. The child was led imperceptibly on to the next stage. In the vertically grouped class system there is a wide range of ability in each class, so each child is working at his own rate and careful records are kept.

We use the *real* situation and our own environment. We try to find topics the children are interested in – such as birthdays, families, T.V. programmes, pets and local journeys. At any time children can be seen moving about the building and grounds – perhaps measuring corridors or wheeling the trundle wheel across the playground. They can be seen in little groups near the gate taking a traffic census. They go shopping for cookery ingredients and check the change and work out the cost.

The children are encouraged to talk, and are encouraged to reason, estimate and calculate. The discussions with the teacher are of immense value – mathematical vocabulary is acquired naturally, as the children have the freedom to live and learn in an environment rich in materials.

Gone are the days when all I needed was a set of arithmetic textbooks, a few tins of counters, a set of exercise books and thirty-six rulers, and gone is my 'Mental, Mechanical and Problem sum' attitude!

The teachers plan to make the classrooms interesting and stimulating yet homely places to work in.

They have a play house – complete with furniture, dolls and dressing-up box; a book corner with many attractive and frequently changed books; a nature table; an investigation table; an armchair and rug and displays of pleasing things – such as objects of natural beauty – perhaps drift wood, shells, teazels, cones, bulrushes or fossils.

We make extensive use of the immediate locality – walking to the bus terminus, the local shop, the library, the railway bridge to watch the London express, the wood yard and the local comprehensive school.

We take bigger outings when we hire a coach and visit the theatre, the cinema, a lake or a farm.

The School Museum Service is invaluable to us and we have had much fun and excitement from the interesting things we have had on loan. Items as diverse as a penny-farthing bicycle, a spinning wheel, cases of butterflies and gaily painted Russian toys have all given us much pleasure.

We keep pets in school – hamsters, goldfish, guinea-pigs, caged birds, terrapins and mice, are all cared for and loved. The children are constantly bringing their pets from home for us to admire – tortoises, puppies, mice and rabbits.

A music table is a constant source of delight in the classroom. There are pitch, percussion and home-made instruments. Here the children can experiment in sounds and rhythms, and, with a little suggestion and guidance they can set their own poems to music, making a satisfying and simple orchestration.

All these various activities and interests are stimulating and exciting. The children are quick to catch the enthusiasm of their teacher and the spontaneous discussions lead to lively written work and vital creative art work.

We are lavish with praise. We mount and display work done by each child. Obviously, not *every* piece of work can be mounted but all work is discussed, and the children know that the teachers are *interested* and keen for each child to progress and succeed.

We converse with the children a great deal – talking is encouraged as many of these little children are almost inarticulate when they enter school.

Physical Education today is vastly different from the PT lessons I used to take when my crisp orders and whistle dictated the order of events. The children, now bare-footed and clad only in vests and pants, think for themselves and make individual responses to ideas of speed, slowness, height, lightness, curling and stretching. They sometimes develop these ideas in groups and a dance or dramatic situation evolves.

The provision of small apparatus gives the children the opportunities to devise fresh and original ways of using these hoops, canes, balls and quoits. The popular large climbing apparatus gives the children chance to experiment daringly and adventurously if they wish.

The plump, awkward girl today finds it quite satisfying to move and work within her own limits – trying out her own ideas of speed or lightness or ball control, without the shame and embarrassment that went with letting the team down, by stumbling, or by dropping the ball, in the strident team games of the old days.

The awarding of stars in return for good work or good behaviour is replaced by constant praise and encouragement. All the children, whatever their ability, have their work quietly discussed as the teacher moves around the various activities. There is always a feeling of close teacher-interest as all the children's efforts are worthy of our attention.

Tests and examinations, that twenty years ago seemed so important, have no place and we no longer use reports.

We meet the parents, hear about the child at home and they, in turn, hear about the child at school. This exchange is far more informative and helpful to both sides than the old style written report.

Parents play a much more definite role in school life now. They attend our assembly once a month and stay on afterwards for refreshments and informal conversations with the staff while the children are out at play. They come into school every Thursday afternoon, for the whole session – on a rota system – and help the teachers, either in the staffroom or in the classroom. They give assistance on walks and outings, they sew, paint and do joinery jobs at home as well as at school.

The contrast between the formal training I received, the formal schools in which I first taught, and the contemporary active school is quite remarkable.

The children are absorbed and involved, working individually or in little groups – artistically, mathematically and scientifically. There is freedom to continue on one job – all day if necessary, there is freedom of movement and freedom to come to terms with and express thoughts in a wealth of different media, and above all, there is the happy, sympathetic and individual relationship between the children and their teacher.

2

CHANGE AS SEEN BY TEACHERS

A head's view of change

A class teacher changes from formal secondary teaching to an 'informal' primary school

Change as seen by a probationer moving from teaching practice to her first teaching post

The changing attitude towards parents

Schools rarely stand still for long periods of time; they either move forward under the impetus of developing ideas backed by the drive of an enlightened Head, or they become dull and fall back. A new Head, anxious to put wrongs to right, may run into difficulties and at worst may be broken by an immovable staff, an older teacher set in his ways may face considerable unhappiness in trying to meet new demands, and a young teacher straight from college often finds a striking difference between his college teaching practice and the responsibilities of facing his first class.

Three teachers; a Head, an experienced teacher who changed from formal secondary teaching to informal primary work, and a beginner have set out their views.

A head's view of change

Most Heads on assuming their headships will find some need for change. The problem is how to bring it about without causing hurt.

First it is important, I think, to try and get older teachers to realise and to anticipate the necessity for change – not merely by saying or implying 'this won't do' but by proving to them and also to oneself that things could be better, that improvements could be made, and that merely because certain things have been done in a certain way for a long time does not mean that they could not be done better in a different way.

It is also important to work constructively and to work from strength wherever possible – personal strength and not merely teaching strength. Amongst our teachers much knowledge and expertise lies untapped and unused – dramatic and musical ability, appreciation of the arts, local knowledge, flower arranging, baking, gardening, bee-keeping and so on. Admittedly some of these interests and hobbies could be too esoteric for use in the junior classroom, but where possible some use should be made of them.

Helping by making physical improvements and alterations to actual teaching conditions and the school environment might come first and is really the easiest task to attempt. A face-lift is both dramatic and encouraging. Alterations of classroom layout should be encouraged, removal of old notice boards (and notices), disposal of old furniture, the display of carefully mounted work, collections of all kinds of interesting objects, and books and equipment that have been chosen with obvious concern – all these things *do* matter and have importance.

Helping the older teachers in their approach to subjects is a more difficult problem. To try to alter the teaching routines of a lifetime is often a seemingly impossible task, and, looking back, I found that all my talk of 'the individual approach' and 'working from experience' held very little meaning until, very gradually, we started what perhaps unfortunately we called our 'activity periods'. These, at first, were no more than an extension of the old Craft lessons, except that the boys and girls were no longer separated. We took art and modelling (I insisted on clay as the medium) and needlework together and proved it could be done without the chaos which had been so confidently forecast. I was now able to ask what else the children could do – so we tried knitting, potato-printing, stick-printing, as further group activities in the same lesson. Good work was being produced, the children were now able to choose their own particular activities and work either as individuals or in a group, they could see each other using different materials, they began to move from group to group, to talk about what they were doing, to discuss problems ('It keeps falling down, sir').

Once this stage was reached the major breakthrough had been made; the children left the four sacred walls of the classroom to sketch without supervision outside in the playground, to garden or to make a traffic census. They created their own music in odd corners of the corridors and they acted and produced their imaginative dramas in the hall, bringing their own costumes and 'props' from home. A wider and wider range of materials was being used in an extremely varied number of ways.

One teacher of many years' experience told me that she had found teaching more interesting and more vital (yet more demanding) over the past three years following a different approach than she had done over the previous twenty. When asked how her children produced needlework, collage and modelling of such high quality, she answered 'They just do it'. I know that really her children are reflecting her own high standards. They are learning from her, just as she has learnt how competent and confident they can be, given the right encouragement.

A second experienced teacher started to take work with a whole range of materials at a later stage when most of the other members of staff had already had some experience. At first she was overwhelmed by it all and we went through a very harrowing time together for about six months as we gradually widened the range. She thought many times that she could not carry on and that the work of her class was 'below standard'. Unfortunately she left the district just as she was finding her feet. I wondered from time to time whether she had liked what we were doing. Three months after she had left she rang me up to ask if she could bring a group of secondary modern slow-learners to the school – 'I really want them to see other children using materials well', she said, 'I'd love to get them interested in doing the things that my previous class were doing.'

An even more difficult problem for many older teachers is to be found in the change in pupil-teacher relationships. It is very difficult for an adult born before the war to appreciate and fully to understand a modern child. Our values, our way of life, our beliefs have changed, even our language is altering. We are hampered by the generation gap, we are hindered by our different upbringing and our unwillingness to show emotion (pleasure, happiness, joy). If we try to show the older teachers that friendliness and an open approach breeds confidence in the children, that the children willingly respond to this, and that this need not lead to a loss of discipline but rather to a new-found respect on both sides, then this I feel is the best we can do.

It is very important that the staff should feel secure and have confidence in the head. Discussions should take place on major matters of policy whenever this is possible, and when decisions have been reached they should be kept to. Changes should be made gradually – we are not a revolutionary people and anything lasting has to grow roots. The

Head must show the way and be prepared to help out at all times. Sometimes this help will be of a practical nature, sometimes the best help he can give is waiting, allowing time for growth and having faith in what he believes is right.

A class teacher changes from formal secondary teaching to an 'informal' primary school

I FOLLOWED a Junior Secondary course in mathematics and geography at my College of Education. During my course I was always adamant that I would go on to teach in a secondary school and my first post was in a small secondary modern school. I taught mathematics and a little geography to first, second and third year children and, being the youngest woman on the staff, some physical education. When I married and moved house I decided to apply for a primary post.

The reasons for this move, which was contrary to my earlier convictions, were numerous. I was by this time far from convinced of the merits of teaching one subject in isolation. There seemed to be little or no transfer of thought from one subject to another. Children who dealt adequately with the metric system in theory in mathematics could not cope with it in practice in the science laboratory. My convictions were strengthened when I saw the progress of the remedial children who joined 3C after two years in a special class where they had been taught all but the practical subjects by one member of staff in an integrated time-table. Their interest, enthusiasm and general knowledge compared more than favourably with the apathetic attitude of the 'brighter' members of 3C who had had two years of a traditional time-table.

In general I felt that the secondary school curriculum that I had experienced was too academic and too far removed from the children's own interests and experience. Despite the fact that very few of the children stayed for a fifth C.S.E. year, the school, like most, was directed towards examinations. Very little was done to involve the children in the work they were doing, indeed, in many cases the schemes of work made involvement virtually impossible. There were discussions and courses on Nuffield Science and Mathematics but the general feeling of groups of teachers seemed against change. I remember being horrified to hear that ninety-five per cent of C.S.E. Mathematics entrants had taken the paper most like G.C.E. This seemed to me to defeat the whole aim of the C.S.E. examination.

My first feelings when faced with a freer time-table and a class of lively talkative eight-year-olds was one of horror. I had never encountered a 'free' approach such as this and even my primary training at college was of a more formal teacher-orientated form.

I began in the only way I knew, which was formally. At first most of the topics were my ideas but gradually I learned to adapt. I discovered the hard way, that if Ian has a new fishing-rod and Jane has brought a goldfish to school the class will do any amount of work on fishing but will show a very half-hearted interest in the Iron Age. I soon found out that if Jimmy was involved in measuring the school hall it wouldn't wait until tomorrow's number lesson.

I was amazed at the capacity for work which some children display when they are really involved in a study of matters which interest them and was astonished at the complexity of the subject matter which they can understand. At first I spent hours planning exactly how we would develop a theme, only to find that some small (to me insignificant) point actually fired their imagination.

I think I have been most impressed by the work I have received in mathematics – naturally one of my main interests. First, on the traditional lines, I have been delighted to see the way in which eight-year-olds have tackled addition and subtraction of length, weight and money as well as number when it has cropped up in a problem. Their 'play' experience has been their only guide. Having experienced eleven-year-olds to whom tables were a guessing game I can appreciate the eight-year-olds' excitement of discovering number patterns and the enjoyment of building up meaningful tables.

Undoubtedly my biggest surprise was when, after a week-end course, I introduced more 'open-ended' problems in shape, space and chance. Here were eight-year-olds explaining to me in their own words discoveries I associated with more advanced study. They talked readily about regular figures, rigid structures and are quick to point out symmetry in their own designs as well as in flowers and leaves.

Throughout the school the children display a deep interest in books of all kinds. They are anxious to use the books and to share with each other the exciting facts discovered or an amusing passage found. The children's interests are so varied and levels of understanding so different that I often wonder how teachers ever managed to keep the class as one without losing those of lower ability or boring the brighter-than-average. Yet when I watch a more gifted child explaining and enthusing about his latest discovery to a child who is not yet able to use the source, I am struck by the enormous social benefits, that the system affords.

All the children from five to eleven derive such enjoyment, interest, knowledge and self-discipline from 'doing', I feel sure that this practical approach cannot cease to be of value at any age. I have been most interested to hear of a more practical approach being used in secondary schools in such subjects as geography and history with the emphasis on local work – surely more meaningful to most of our twelve-year-olds than studying the southern continents.

The only worries I have about this 'modern' approach concern the transfer of children to the secondary schools which still, in the main, employ a formal time-table. I feel that some children must suffer from the change in methods and I would like to see more co-operation between junior and secondary schools in local areas.

In conclusion I would like to say that I have never re-gretted my change from secondary to junior school teaching. Whilst I find the work far more demanding the approach is far more in tune with present-day demands.

Change as seen by a probationer moving from teaching practice to her first teaching post

I WONDER how many young teachers, fresh from college, arrive at their first appointment on the first day of the autumn term unconvinced? Unconvinced that is of the way in which they are going to teach the children in their care, because they are unconvinced of any philosophy lying behind their actions, be it radical, progressive, liberal or even plain conservative. They have talked, they have argued, they have discussed, they have intellectualised, they have written essays; yet they do not *know* because they have not been in enough classroom situations to be able to evaluate what is the best way of providing an authentic education for the children they are about to teach.

Is it any wonder that the vast number of teachers as soon as they begin their careers resort to those methods with which they are most familiar? – that is, the methods by which they themselves were taught, perhaps with a few liberal modifications here and there? How many times did I hear on my own course: 'Well it's all right for these lecturers trying to convince us with all these modern methods but they don't have to cope with forty children.' Those students were probably never given the chance to be convinced in a favourable situation where the ideas that tutors bandied about were actually worked out in practice.

If you have ever worked in a strictly rigid primary school, streamed A, B and C, where desks are in rows and must stay like that at all costs, and where talking is prohibited unless the teacher asks you a question, you will appreciate the difficulty of a student experimenting with ideas he or she has learned about informal education. Faced with tutors who at least expect to see that some of their ideas have got through to the student he is placed in an intolerable position.

In such a school my final practice took place. At a preliminary interview the Head of the school impressed upon me the insignificant role of the student on teaching practice, told me to take no notice of my tutors, who knew nothing of real teaching, and then took me to a classroom where a bored teacher was sitting at a desk at the front of the class, shouting occasional threats to an equally bored class who were doing a mathematics exercise. Apart from three days when my class teacher took over another class while their teacher went on a course, I was never allowed to teach the whole class for a full day and even the three days I was given were bestowed on me as a great honour by the Head. This was my final practice before having a class of my own for a whole year and yet for only three full days was I allowed to take the class on my own all day.

My tutors must have known that my ideas of teaching were far from conservative; they knew I was taking up an appointment in a progressive school, yet I was given a school where I could do no group work let alone individual work, where I was not allowed to do art in the classroom and where the children could not borrow books from the school library to do work for me because they already had at home the one or two books allowed on their tickets. When I complained to the P.E. specialist that in a movement lesson the children couldn't even manage to move into a space she replied: 'We don't have any of those modern methods here!' Three weeks out of the six I was there were taken up with one week's holiday, one week of examinations (eleven of them), and one week's rehearsal for speech day. With this lack of experience I was to take up in a term's time my first job as a professional teacher working in a school which I knew had a reputation for using child-centred methods and using them well.

But I am one of the lucky few who have emerged happily from our hazardous and inadequate system, because I myself attended an excellent informal primary school and because I went out of my way as a student to visit and work in good child-centred primary schools. My bizarre experiences on teaching practice only served to reinforce my belief that children should be the agents of their own learning and that only when children are completely absorbed in what they are doing can a teacher begin to feel satisfied. Many of my contemporaries were less fortunate. We learnt from notes but we did not learn to think because we were not put into situations where we had to do so. Those of us who had this kind of experience will produce new generations of children who do not adequately learn how to think and who are bored by what they are doing.

I cannot stress enough that if the colleges of education and the university institutes wish to inculcate change in our education system they must do so by putting their students in the way of the change which is already taking place, to convince them by experience 'at the grass roots'. Only if more lecturers do this can they safely afford to theorise. At the end of his final teaching practice at the school where I work a student said to me, 'I can honestly say that I have learned more in these few weeks than in all the time I have been in college'.

Of course he had. He was working with one of my talented colleagues – but he is one of the minority. Many of the students in training never come into contact with talented teachers in exciting classroom situations. Students should be in schools at least one full day each week, not just on three teaching practices in three years and an odd visit now and then. I await with open arms the day when I can have students working with me from local colleges as often as possible. The children love to have extra adults in the classroom. They know that with nearly forty children I can give very little time to each of them as individuals but with an extra one or two adults they can share their achievements and difficulties so much more easily and love to do so. The children benefit enormously and the students learn so much in a situation where they don't have to grapple with structural difficulties but can concentrate on the children themselves as they battle to make sense of the situations with which they are presented. It is high time that both the schools and the colleges recognised their complementary needs and tapped the gloriously rich resources which could so easily be made available to both parties.

The changing attitude towards parents

IT IS not so very long ago that one of my staff at a previous school said 'These mothers are getting such a nuisance – crowding round the school door in the mornings. There is no need for it. They ought to stand outside the railings.'

When I came to my present school, I found that parents dare not come near the building, but had to say 'Goodbye' to their infant son or daughter at the gate, and wave as the child toddled down the path to the door. No teacher was allowed to be approached by a parent. Permission to speak must be first sought through the Headmistress, and if approved a conversation could be held.

It seemed as though teachers generally regarded parents as an unavoidable nuisance to be ignored if possible and not allowed to interfere in any way with the real business of life!

Times have changed. In the last few years there have been great developments in home/school relationships.

At the beginning of the day, and at the end of the afternoon the school is buzzing with mothers, fathers and pre-school children. Greetings, remarks about the weather, smiles and nods abound, children take mothers into the classrooms to see the paintings or booklets made yesterday. Often, quite unasked, a willing mother, with a few minutes to spare, will help set out the various materials, or sit down in the Book Corner to look at her child's favourite book.

In the term prior to admittance, the mother is invited to bring the child to school on two or three occasions and to spend some time in the classroom. When the child does commence, he comes for mornings only for the first four weeks. Mothers collect the children at twelve o'clock and we have found that very good teacher/parent relations are established in these early days. With vertical grouping – there are only a few admissions per class, and mothers often chat with the teacher for a few minutes when they come to collect the children at noon.

On the last Friday in every month we have our Family Assembly. Parents, pre-school children, aunts, grandparents, in fact anyone interested, comes to join us in our daily worship. They stay on for tea, biscuits and a chat with each other and with the staff. We have been delighted to find this is a very worthwhile social gathering. The teachers move among the parents – from table to table – greeting them and chatting. Often little problems and worries are discussed at this time, and the mothers seem really to enjoy the simple little service and the friendly party afterwards.

During last year we started having mothers in school to help every Thursday afternoon. They either worked in the staffroom or in the hall. They did sewing, painted house-corner furniture, painted art easels, washed aprons, cot blankets, doll's clothes, they ironed fabrics from the fabric boxes, made booklets, sharpened pencils, etc. So many mothers wished to come that rotas had to be devised – so their turn came round only once or twice a term.

At first the staff were naturally a little shy about having mothers in school but the benefits soon became apparent; the eagerness of parents to be involved, children's delight in having 'Mum' in school, the definite practical help to teachers, help with chores which allowed more time to be spent with the children, and the friendlier atmosphere between the community and the school. A collection in the area raised £31 to enable us to buy a paddling pool. Fathers mend toys and do joinery jobs, Mothers knit and sew at home.

Now, this school year – we have made further progress. We asked ourselves, why limit this valuable help to one afternoon and why not involve parents more, within the classrooms? There is nothing to hide or be ashamed of – so why give the mothers jobs only outside the classroom, and why not give more opportunities for parents to be *with* the children? Why restrict them to little chores? Let us do *more* to break down the mystique that surrounds the word 'school'.

Now parents are in school every day. Each class teacher has a list of mothers who are available, and she devises her own rota. Some mothers come in for half a day once a week, others come in for half a day once a fortnight.

The kind of help the mothers give is still of a definite practical nature – but they are becoming much more integrated into school life.

For example, they help the children wash their painting materials and their clay utensils, they help thread needles, keep an eye on the weighing and mixing of cookery ingredients, sharpen pencils, look at a picture book with one or two young children, help to pack away equipment and set out what is needed next, bandage a cut finger or a grazed knee, help with tight trousers or awkward tights, washing and drying in the cloakrooms, help with dressing after PE and have a readiness to give a word of comfort and a hug when it is needed.

Already we are looking ahead to the time when two teachers and two groups of children will share the same large working area, and mothers will be a most welcome feature of our new plans.

Of course, it is inevitable that some parents do not come to Family Assembly or show any desire to help in school. In fact, they do not seem to take much interest in school or in their child's progress. However, they *do* come to jumble sales and perhaps the garden party. They are not reluctant to come into school with late meals money, or a request for help in filling in forms. So friendly contact is made, and, whenever possible, a conversation is held concerning the child. The odd remark such as 'Oh – before you go – do come and see what John did yesterday. He is so proud of it!' can often lead to an awareness of our concern and affection for their child.

A side-issue, and one we did not expect, is the role the school is now seeming to assume in this sprawling suburb. The area, though fairly new, has been very badly planned, and there is no centre, no heart, to this vast estate. There is no square where housewives can wheel their prams, sit in the sun, have coffee or meet each other. There is no restaurant or tea shop, and it seems that the school, through its Family Assembly and its invitation to mothers to help, is filling a social need in the community.

3

SOME EXAMPLES OF FINDING OUT

Finding out about shadows
The slow learner's writing
Mathematical advance
Starting to read

> 'From the beginning of his education the child should experience the joy of discovery'
>
> A. N. WHITEHEAD

The main change which has taken place in the last twenty-five years in our classroom methods and approach is, as the Plowden Committee put it, from 'being told' to 'finding out'.

It would need a whole book to describe how this change took place, first in art, then in physical education, English and mathematics, and how 'environmental studies came into existence. It was not simply that barriers between the subjects were broken down, but that 'experiences' were fed into the minds of the children who reacted by positive inquiry and investigation.

Once initiative and decision making were left more in the hands of the children the teachers themselves began to learn from them.

The following chapter consists of three accounts of ways in which children enlightened their teachers about the whole learning process.

The first, entitled 'Finding Out about Shadows', is an account of scientific 'learning by discovery'.

The second, 'The Slow Learner's Writing', made clear to

an incredulous staff that a semi-literate child may nevertheless be capable of a sensitive use of words.

The third, 'Mathematical Advance', tells of a child who though capable of unusual mathematical thought had been held back by traditional teaching and how eventually the newer ways released him and allowed him to go ahead.

The final section, 'Learning to read', has been included because the topic is perennially green.

Finding out about shadows

OBSERVATION led us to work on shadows. The little ones in the first year play around with their shadows, finding out what each shadow will do and what makes it. All this is done quite informally out in the yard when, because of their excitement and interest, the children are voluble. Simon said, 'The sun shines on the ground and makes it light, but it can't shine through us so it makes dark patches. Really you get the sun, then us and the shadow on the other side.' When the teacher followed this up with, 'Can you lose your shadow?' the answers came fast – 'Yes, in the shade of the school, in the shadow of the wall, in the shade of a tree – it moves if the wind blows the tree, it fades when the sun goes in.' Whereupon Michael said, 'They've all gone into one big shadow. I know! The cloud has gone over the sun and made a big shadow so the sun can't shine on us.'

Eventually we draw round each other's shadows and find that all face the same way and when we come out later discover they have both moved and altered in size. Michael must have found drawing round the whole shadow rather tedious for he said, 'Could we just stand a stick or something on the ground, then we'd only have to draw a line.'

After further discussion the children reached the following conclusions: light makes shadows of things, so does the fire, a candle, a torch, the lamp and the moon. Simon quietly added, 'Night is a shadow really, because the sun is shining on the world and can't shine through it, so the other side of the world is in the shadow – that's why it's night at one side and day at the other.'

By the time we reach the fourth year shadows have become a science.

I stood waiting for the sun to shine. It was just ten o'clock and from behind a cloud popped the sun. I looked on to the floor and although the clocks had been put forward one hour the sun made the shadow of the jumping stand exactly on the nine o'clock shadow for Friday, but now it was ten o'clock. We can change the clock so that it is light for an hour more at night, but we cannot change the sun.

We graph the shadows through the day and find there is a relationship as the shadow graph has a constant shape. Knowing this, we can now plot a graph and realise if and where our measuring has gone wrong. We can use the shadow graph as a shadow clock (sundial) and later as a shadow compass when we realise that the line of the shortest shadow points north and south.

Yesterday we put a shadow stick outside in the playground and measured the length of the shadow every half-hour from 9 a.m. to 4 p.m. The length of the shadows decreased from 24 ft. $\frac{1}{2}$ in. until 2 p.m. when the length started to increase. When we finished measuring the shadows at 4 p.m. the length was 12 ft. 8 in. Today we noticed that the shadows were in the same place at the same time as the chalk marks we had drawn yesterday. The shadows turned around the stick just like the hands do on a clock. We also noticed that when the shadow was half-way between two of the chalk marks the time was also half-way between the full hour and the half-hour. We then knew we had found a way of telling the time, a sort of shadow clock or clock sundial.

SOME EXAMPLES OF FINDING OUT

Still only using the school as our environment we progress to using the globe as a miniature world and the projector as a miniature sun and we set out to find if we can tell the time by the position of the shadows as we could by the actual cast shadow in the playground. We had already found out about day and night using our minor world and time was our next task.

We experimented with a little pill of plasticine on the globe's surface, putting it in different positions in the northern hemisphere and noting the shadows formed while in each position as the earth rotated. Stephen summed up the procedure in a few words:

All this meant that the shadows in different parts of the Northern Hemisphere (we have not yet tried the south) behaved in the same way as each other.

Paul suggested that we try the plasticine mountain on the equator and this caused quite a stir of excitement. Audrey tried to express what she considered the sundial would be like at the equator resulting from this experiment.

At the equator because their shadows do not behave like ours, they will have to have a different sundial. Our shadows move round so our sundials are made round. I think the sundials at the equator will be long and thin with a stick in the middle.

Stephen progressed even further and found that the noon-day shadow (shortest) points due north and south which is equivalent to the lines which run north and south on the globe – hence he could now find this relationship and took great pleasure in finding times in different parts of the world when it is noon-day here.

Susan worked on shadow lengths taken at the same time daily:

I measured as many eleven o'clock shadows of the 'jumping stand' as I could throughout the year. I then drew the angle drawings of the shadows and graphed the angle against the date and the length against the date. I have noticed with my scale drawings that the shorter the shadow measures the bigger the angle is. In a year the sun comes low in the winter months making shadows really long but in the summer months the sun is high up in the sky casting only short shadows.

Our shadow work and environment led us into further interesting mathematics work in finding the height of buildings from cast shadows.

At 10.35 a.m. the yard stick's shadow measured 2 ft. 8 in. and we found the relationship of the shadow to the stick as 8/9. while at the same time the school's shadow was 31 ft. 2 in., so we inferred that this would have the same relationship of 8/9. So the school would be

$$31 \text{ ft. } 2 \text{ in.} \div 8/9 = 3 \text{ ft. } 10\tfrac{3}{4} \text{ in.} \times 9 = 35 \text{ ft. } 0\tfrac{3}{4} \text{ in.}$$

The slow learner's writing

OUR less able children wrote slowly and with great effort. With such children we found it very hard, at first, to resist the impulse towards the traditional corrections which are so closely bound up with our sense of professional duty and responsibility. I suppose that we had been working primarily to try to improve technique, for they were not expected to have anything to say – The child who cannot read, cannot write. Now one or two teachers really began to look at their work for its content and when they had 'interpreted' it they would excitedly bring pieces to me with 'Who do you think has written this?' Then the child had the thrill of reading his work to the class for the first time, or of hearing it read by his teacher.

When the following pieces were being written the teacher

would help when requested – usually with a spelling. Far more help would be given before the fair copy was made. An eight-year-old wrote about the wind and rain:

I gow red with the cold wind. It wase bluwing at my legs. The rine bluw at mye fase. It cept bluwing my y ud dawn. The ren wase awnsing on the flor and wetting my legs. Suwe I went home and got driyed but it was haw yous. It started agan. It fellt like sumething from a nother planet. The rane was batering at my head. When I trid to run I fellt num I slip on my fase. I was shivering m hows was hurt. When I first got out it was bitter and chilly.

[I go red with the cold wind. It was blowing at my legs. The rain blew at my face. It kept blowing my hood down. The rain was bouncing off the floor and wetting my legs. So I went home and got dried but it was no use. It started again. It felt like something from another planet. The rain was battering at my head. When I tried to run I felt numb, I slipped on my face. I was shivering, my nose was hurt. When I first got out it was bitter and chilly.]

We found this sentence in one piece of work and when we had read it we were more sympathetic towards this ten-year-old and his dreamy ways:

'I have to sleap on the sofa and for ocloc in the morning my farther waks me up and I hay to go the sealeep on my dad bed.'

[I have to sleep on the sofa and at four o'clock in the morning my father wakes me up and I have to go to sleep in my dad's bed.]

A nine-year-old boy who had great difficulty with his writing produced the following sentences:

The gerees is wet and silver and the fog is gost disappearing in the sun lit an huw wald is cumming cowed are on the fens and engs it is lik pet and beb cwiwt and silet.

[The grass is wet and silver and the fog is just disappearing in the sunlight. A new world is coming. Cobwebs are on the fences and hedges. It feels dead quiet and silent.]

The fog is glomey liyck black smorg. Lamps glering throw the smorg. invisibl figers futing like elicoters. thro the dirock and glome fog it glisens laye the golbnfleys it movs impasele past.

[The fog is gloomy like black smoke. Lamps glaring through the smoke. Invisible figures floating like helicopters through the dark and gloomy fog. It glistens like the golden fleece. It moves impatiently past.]

The wint is saying the winter is cumeing and all the squirrels abawt thrling with friyt the trees get rid of theer onley bytey the niyt lovs impasele across its glomey medows winters coming cots and scars the old wold is come dacto use the winte movs sloley pist snow flos liy fethers of an egel.

[The wind is saying the winter is coming and all the squirrels scattering about with fright. The trees get rid of their only beauty. The night moves impatiently across its gloomy meadows. Winter is coming. Coats and scarves. The old world has come back to us. Winter moves slowly past. Snow falls like the feathers of an eagle.]

After we had taken children across the road to see the local fair being set up, a very 'slow learning' ten-year-old wrote:

The fair's a skelinto of wood. It's sad. Then it slwly grows, the noise grows. Eech clater bang bang is another bone in the skelinton, the flesh apers, cloth, canvas, then the blod is atracted by all the marveles colours. Blod which is people they all flock to it. The skilton of wood is a skelinton of happiness, now the generator pumps away. it stops and the blod gos, the flesh comes off the skelinto bones snap.

[The fair's a skeleton of wood. It's sad. Then it slowly grows. Each clatter bang bang is another bone in the skeleton, the flesh appears, cloth, canvas, the blood is attracted by all the marvellous colours. Blood which is people they all flock to it. The skeleton of wood is a skeleton of happiness, now the generator pumps away. It stops and the blood goes, the flesh comes off the skeleton bones snap.]

By pieces of work such as these we were made aware that our 'less ables' had powerful and sensitive ideas of their own and that we could help them to express them. Once a teacher finds an unusual or stirring phrase that shows that the child has had his eyes opened by imaginative personal writing the child usually goes on to produce more. Our most important job with the less able is to rid them of the effects of failure. Movement and drama, art and craft had helped considerably in this. Now we were finding that the nourishment and exercise of the imagination through writing providing another way to develop the child's capacity. In some cases their reading improved quickly.

Mathematical advance

IT IS sometimes suggested that, in laying emphasis on less formal approaches to work in mathematics in the primary school particularly, benefits may be obtained for average and less able children but that the boy or girl with exceptional mathematical talent is not given full opportunity to develop

Jeremy was such a boy, who transferred to a junior school where practical activities and individual approaches to mathematics were encouraged. He had already had two years' experience of very formal work in his previous school and had derived satisfaction from habitually obtaining full marks for all his sums. On arriving at his new school at the age of nine, he was at first somewhat bewildered by the different emphasis, but after an initial period where he was allowed to maintain his security by continuing familiar work, he was gradually encouraged to strike off in new directions on his own.

He was soon able to talk about what he had been doing. Shortly after his tenth birthday he described his work as follows:

I saw in a book about there being a relationship between the squares of whole numbers so I wrote down the cubes of all the numbers from 1 to 20 and decided to see if I could find a similar relationship. First I found the differences between them, and then the differences between the differences. I found I got part of a six times table. So I thought that I ought to be able to work back from this and I carried on the table starting with the differences between the differences and so got the cube of 21, the cube of 22 and so on.

He set out his work:

		DIFFERENCE	DIFFERENCE
1^3	1	7	12
2^3	8	19	18
3^3	27	37	24
4^3	64	61	
5^3	125		

He eventually went on to generalise his answer and said, 'I thought that this showed that there was a way of working out the cube of any number from the cube of the previous number and I found that if any number was called 'n' the cube of the next number would be

$$n^3+3n^2+3n+1.$$

Jeremy had also developed his own work on 'Magic Square', finally constructing his own squares of 16 or 17 rows and columns and explaining to a visitor, 'It is very easy to work out once you've understood the pattern.'

One cannot help contrasting the way in which Jeremy had been allowed to think along his own lines and develop his own mathematical ideas with the way in which his previous mathematical education had been restricted to routine work with arithmetical processes – and also to contrast the demands made upon him in his new way of working with the former situation where he always obtained full marks without really being asked to exert any mathematical effort in his thinking.

Starting to read

MUCH is said about 'reading readiness' – the point at which a child is really ready to read – and it varies from child to child. However, it can be very tardy in arriving if an unfertile environment is provided. As the right soil and a good climate enable a plant to grow easily and sturdily, so an encouraging atmosphere and a good, carefully fostered environment can encourage a child's desire to read.

A young child's first interest is himself. His next interest is his family and home. Then comes his immediate environment – his classroom and friends. Before reading and writing comes speech, and we must use the above interests to help speech, which, when a child first comes to school, is often poor and monosyllabic, particularly if he hears little good speech at home.

Talking to each other, to the teacher, to anyone in school is encouraged. Experiences are shared in conversation. What seems a small happening to us is of enormous importance in a child's world. Questions subtly asked draw out more talk, and 'Let's draw it' leads to expression on paper, maybe by a teacher if a child is shy, or by the child if he is more forthcoming. Before long 'Shall we write it?' leads to large writing by the teacher under the picture on a large sheet of paper. We add to these sheets as often as news is forthcoming. Pictures and short sentences accumulate. Each page has special significance to someone, and others remember some picture or some incident and link it with the written sentence. 'John has a new red jersey' is of considerable importance to John. Soon this collection is a book to be taken down and looked at, not as a class but by a group and a teacher and then by individuals who perhaps then read to each other. Other books follow and since they are all 'personal' they sustain the interest.

Painting and drawing are used to stimulate language. Sometimes a child will talk as he paints. Sometimes he will tell about his paintings afterwards. It will give him much pleasure if the teacher writes 'David painted this big aeroplane'. He will refer to it again and again. He will take his friends to see it and will 'read' it to them. They will be encouraged to 'read' it. Each is helping the others.

At the same time the teacher will at some time each day be telling and reading stories and showing pictures. The children will be encouraged to realise that pleasure comes from books. Many may never have seen their parents reading books. The choosing of these is of the utmost importance. Good illustrations, good colours, attractive layout, good printing – all make a book a thing of pleasure and a desirable thing to have. As well as using books in school children and parents are encouraged to belong to the local library. Our public libraries are excellent and the children proudly bring their library books to school. Many of these are read to the children and many are things of real beauty. Brian Wildsmith's books are always loved for their wonderful illustrations, and when they are told that Brian belongs to Yorkshire as we do and doesn't live too far away they seek them out and enjoy them. Parents very often begin to enjoy books as much as their children, and the more interested ones come in and talk about them.

The free use of a great variety of materials in the school helps discussion and later on writing. Clay is used a great deal. The younger children soon begin to find out what they can do with it.

The teachers will help them to experiment with this new material, working alongside them, explaining what it can do, encouraging them to find out, and all the time talking, questioning 'What will you need to do next?' 'How many legs will that elephant have?' 'How can we make this clay softer?' Conversation is important and this is where other adults can help a great deal. Talk in the house corner flows freely. In time children learn to communicate and to express thoughts increasingly clearly.

The school building itself is used from the beginning. When the new children have been at school a little while they go with their teacher to see the rest of the building and the people in it. They see what others do and make, and talk to them. They explore the outside of the school and talk about it. In turn this leads to more pictures, more writing by the teacher, more 'reading' by the children.

Later they will go to the small park nearby and explore there. The expedition is talked about, enjoyed again, painted, drawn and remembered. Quite often we look for something special, 'See how many different shapes of leaves you can find.' 'We found five shapes of leaves' – these may be drawn as a record. Everything is used to help children to think, to talk, to record in some way.

When a teacher considers the time has come to introduce a printed reading book to an individual child or group of children they will already be very familiar with the story it tells and will be able to recognise many of the words because they have already been encountered. The excitement of being able to 'read' quickly through a first reading book and thus feel a real sense of achievement cannot be over-estimated. The teacher's skill lies in choosing the right moment for its introduction. When this happens too soon and a child is left worrying his way laboriously from page 1 (and all too often turning back to page 1 daily) with the book becoming soiled and torn, both time and motivation are wasted.

'Hear me read', 'It's my turn', may prove a challenging situation to a teacher without any ancillary help but is rewarding proof of her initial training of the children.

Writing goes side by side with reading and again choosing the right moment is important. Each child has his personal book in which he draws and describes his picture in writing probably decipherable only by the teacher. Each child reaches this stage in his own time. It varies from child to child but often it does not come without all the stimuli that a teacher can use. Everything is pressed into service to help the child's speech, communication, reading and writing.

At about this stage children begin to notice the patterns of words and to be able to pick out identical words. They enjoy seeing how speedily they can do it – 'This word is "ship" – can you find another one that says "ship"? Thus repetition can be made interesting.

Flash cards and similar games are enjoyed. Later, sounds come; 'That one is in my name', they say, and letters are learned. These come last in the mechanics of reading, but come they must if the child is to help himself. As the children become more aware of others and have more interests apart from their personal ones they begin to explore more and to enjoy more complicated and diverse things. Imagination is developing. Things brought into the classroom stimulate their imagination. Collections are made, talked about, written about, speculated on. Books now begin to have their uses for reference. If a child's personal interests can be discovered he will go to a great deal of trouble to read a book about them. All that happens in the school and the community around him, as well as things happening farther afield, can be used now as items for reading and writing interests. A visit by the West Riding Orchestra is written about individually, illustrated and made into a class book which they read and re-read with joy because they made it. The moon landing was an important event which appealed enormously to children, to be read about, illustrated and discussed. Seasons, festivals, gatherings, performances, etc., can provide material. The Christmas story never fails to be enjoyed, wondered at and recounted in pictures and writing. Simple expeditions afford further material – even if it is only to see how the large grass-cutter works. Both good recording and imaginative writings are important. Learning how to do things, baking and reading recipes in order to do so, is invariably interesting. In short, everything can be used to stimulate the desire and the need to read and write.

Reading and writing grow from interests fostered carefully at all times by the teacher, centred on the child, himself, his family, his interests, his school and his surroundings. Without stimulation reading would be slow to begin. Without the use of all available media it would be laborious. Without talk and interest it would be stilted and without imagination it would be sterile.

4

WHAT SORT OF AN AREA DO YOU TEACH IN?

What if your school is in an old run-down urban area?
It might be more difficult on a new Coal Board estate.
The dormitory suburb isn't without its problems
What about teaching in a village school?
We are in an old building and we have no space

'Unfortunately when all has been said, the conditions
under which the work has to be done affect the possibility
of doing the work'

EDWARD THRING

*Teaching and learning are bound to be affected by the social
conditions in which the pupils live. The village school, the
urban school, the suburban school, the school on the new estate
and the school in the slum; all have their advantages and disadvantages.*

*One of the most deplorable facts of the otherwise splendid era
of post-war school building is that the last children to leave
the worst areas are very often those who stand most in need of the
exhilaration that a fine new building can bring.*

*The purpose of this chapter is to set out the problems of the
different areas and to describe ways in which enlightened and
eager staffs have sought to make the most of the sad old buildings
in which they had to work.*

*Incidentally, an important point well worth making is that
over the last twenty-five years in the county in which this book
has been produced, much of the most outstanding work has*

*been done in socially poor if not deprived areas and much of it in
lamentably inadequate buidings.*

What if your school is in an old run-down urban area?

*Two Heads were asked to give their views on the difficulties
of running a school in a poor social area; the first in an old,
the second in a new building.*

IN AN OLD BUILDING

TEACHING in a mining area where the majority of the
children in these days of affluence are now materially
quite well provided for, but in varying degrees are socially
deprived, presents a constant challenge.

How do we define a poor social background in terms of
this particular school? The environment – a sprawling urban
area, surrounded by undistinguished though pleasant rural
scenery, but presenting in itself a drab and grimy picture.
Pit headgear and slag heaps punctuate the sky-line, and
narrow streets of houses, many pre-1914 in origin, crowd
around a school built at the turn of the century.

Apart from one cinema, the only entertainment is that
provided by the numerous bingo halls, working-men's clubs
and public houses; the only cultural amenity the public
library. In most of the homes there is a dearth of reading
matter and what there is is totally lacking in quality. Very
few families are attached even loosely to any religious body.
Some of the children come from broken homes, and ironi-
cally, many from materially good homes are deprived of
parental interest and care, since to create this affluent
situation the mother is out at work or at the bingo session
when the children are at home.

The problem then, was how to compensate for this lack
of beauty – how to combat this harsh, unlovely environ-

ment, where the prevailing philosophy of aggressive self-interest is epitomised by the daily procession of grim-faced women to the bingo 'casino'.

The first essential was to create inside school an environment which would compensate visually for the ugliness outside. In spite of the many limitations of an old building, badly sited on a busy main road, facing north and with every window framing a view of bricks and mortar, it was possible to create a place of colour and interest. The arrangement and display of natural materials, the arrangeent of furniture, the careful mounting and presentation of children's work, the introduction of living things – even of simple ones such as tropical fish and budgerigars – all combined to produce stimulating and exciting surroundings. In order to widen the children's experience of natural and man-made beauty, visits were organised to most of the places of historical, artistic or natural interest within reach. The spontaneous delight of children seeing Fountains Abbey for the first time was something not to be forgotten.

But more than all these undoubted necessities, I believe it is essential to create a way of life in school based on caring for and concern for others, to try to make not merely a school community but in fact a 'caring' community. This then was the task, to establish the knowledge that each child was an important individual, valued as a member of the community and for his or her contribution to the life of the school, and the encouragement of the natural consequence of this, a generous and kindly attitude to each other. But thought and care for others cannot grow where there is insecurity and lack of confidence. This is seen most clearly in children who are severely deprived, as for instance four sisters, members of a large family, well-known as a problem family, and all four in school at the time same. These children were closely linked by a strong bond of family affection and an equally strong family suspicion of society. In school this took the form of stealing, lying and vicious fighting. It was a slow and often disheartening process building up in these girls the belief that they were valued and that each one had something to contribute to the life of the school which was accepted by everybody. It was not a question simply of trying to supply material deficiencies. Library books were torn up by the babies at home and such things as socks, dresses and cardigans given by compassionate neighbours were eaten by the dog or lost in the *mêlée* of old rags which served for bedding. Some other ways of building self-confidence were needed. One of the greatest compensations for all the children, but particularly for children such as these four sisters, was the opportunity they were given to express themselves in dance and drama. For the many who found it difficult to communicate in speech and writing there was this joyful release in another medium. The limits of their horizons were extended. They explored the excitements of music, and imagination, and as they gradually gained in confidence they became happily integrated in the group. I think here of Carol, thin, poorly clad, unhappy and oppressed by the responsibilities of 'mothering' four equally miserable younger children. Withdrawn and often temperamental in the classroom she became a changed child in the movement lesson. Her sad little face lost its hunted look as she forgot herself in the joy of moving and in the happiness of being one of a group.

The class dance dramas which the older children create are the result and revelation of their attitude of concern for others. The most eagerly anticipated event in the life of the school took place in the Parish Church at Christmas. There, in surroundings of great beauty, the top class children told in speech and dance their own interpretation of the story of the Nativity. Every member of the class took part and their dignity and absorption was an unforgettable experience.

These are but some of the ways in which we can overcome and compensate for the disadvantages of a poor social background. As the children grew in self-assurance and poise, their ability to take control of a situation was seen in all aspects of the life of the school, be it conducting a morning Assembly with reverence and relevance, organising a truly original and creative concert at the end of the school year, or merely handling the day-to-day encounters of school relationships.

My school was in a new building in an industrial area. The parents of all our children were semi- or unskilled workers, not one was a white-collared worker. Many came from homes with one or several of the following social problems:

(a) Family with a criminal – prison – record.
(b) Broken home.
(c) Mother a prostitute.
(d) No regularity of any sort within the home, e.g. bed-times, meal-times, pocket-money, discipline.
(e) Lack of any educational material in the home, e.g. books, paints, even pencil or paper.
(f) Lack of cleanliness.
(g) Cases of incest.
(h) Lack of any conversation or discussion within the home.
(i) 'Work-shy' fathers.

When I came to the school it had on roll 230 children aged five to eleven-plus. They had been transferred from a very overcrowded, very old junior school, and a similarly over-crowded infant school. The majority of the juniors had come from C classes in this junior school.

On the first morning the children arrived, many were dirty, clothes were torn, jeans were usually torn and patched and on the first inspection 120 children had nits and many had sores. By far the worst feature was the fact that many of the children looked ashamed, and so did their parents.

I had a terrific advantage in having a beautiful new building, surrounded, at that time, by fields and farmland. I had quickly to give the children a feeling of pride in this building, and to ensure that it was kept beautiful. By giving the children a stake in keeping one part – their own desks – tidy, polished and unmarked – by fine displays and constant reminders we soon established this pride. We were determined to get the parents with us and they were invited to come and see the building even before the children came. It was stressed to the parents that this was their building, and would be used by their children. This constant stress on care and pride in the building seemed to work. In eight years only one window was broken, and that was an accident. There was only one case of writing on lavatory walls. The re-decoration of the school was delayed for twelve months because of the excellent condition of the fabric.

My first movement lesson gave me a great shock; the children changed – thirty-six in all – there were thirty-six pairs of filthy feet, and filthy underclothes. Changing for movement became a daily occurrence. Feet were inspected very regularly. After a short time, feet became clean, and strangely enough underclothes became much whiter.

Cases of nits decreased from 120 cases on the first head inspection to three hardened cases after a year. The school nurse co-operated in this sphere.

As far as general dress was concerned and after one or two arguments we insisted on boys wearing short trousers and after some time these were accepted by parents as normal, and became a tradition. By constant reminders, good examples and building up a pride in themselves, I can quite honestly say that there wasn't a cleaner or prouder group of children. I must also add that gradually the parents had faith in the staff, which is absolutely essential and often takes several years to achieve.

The two things I have mentioned so far are questions of standards. I feel very strongly that we must stress standards in all things – in dress, in speech, in work and the way it is presented. Many children, if not surrounded by high standards, if not constantly encouraged to aim higher, will never have the opportunity of seeing, or knowing, what decent standards are. Before we can ask children to raise their standards of work they must have a real pride in it and to enable children to develop this pride they must first be successful. To ensure success the curriculum must be very wide and the artistic side – music, art, movement – must be treated not as a frill but as important as mathematics and English. The relationship between teacher and child, and child and child, must be one of consideration and respect, not one of familiarity. The work should be concrete and opportunity given for the children to use their senses, to see, to touch, hear, and smell. In education we often introduce children to abstractions far too soon, long before they have sufficient experiences on which to base them.

With success the children will become more secure, this will lead to confidence and this confidence will often quickly spread from the narrow sphere in which they were first successful. Underlying everything must be love, love in its true sense. Within our school we established love, security and success. The staff were willing to show their fairness, and their care. This was shown in many ways, by creating a homely atmosphere, by being ready for the children each morning, by being prepared to help for a few minutes after 4 p.m. We had breaks, but were not tied to bells. The teachers ensured that whatever work the children did was well presented, or marked with care. The classrooms were always lively, interesting places, and displays were tastefully arranged. As a result of this obvious care not only did the children respond, but the once belligerent parents became our friends and helpers. They arranged, quite on their own, coffee evenings, etc., and raised lots of money for school funds. Any school functions always attracted at least ninety per cent of the parents.

Parents developed a great faith and trust in us. I well remember when one of them sought my help. She was expecting her ninth child. She didn't want more and it was to the school that she came for help and advice.

It might be more difficult on a new Coal Board estate

I HAVE spent the whole of my teaching life so far, in two mining communities, and how different these communities are. I find it quite incredible that two mining areas, so near together, could be so different.

The first twenty-six years of my career were spent in what one might call a small old, run-down, or running down, mining area – a small township where the pit stacks came down to within yards of the back doors of many houses and where on a breezy day everything was covered with a film of red shale dust, so that one seemed to be walking on a sugar-sprinkled floor.

But this was a place with strong traditions, deep roots, and a great feeling for 'the family'. Grandma and granddad lived round the corner, aunts, uncles, and cousins lived up the road, or in the next street, and everyone knew everyone else.

There was an enormous respect for the school – it was part of the place. Mum and dad went there when they were young, and often grandma and granddad too. It was a place where people were always made welcome, and no one was afraid to come in for a chat. Coming, as they did, from a stable, settled community, where the roots went very deep, and entering a school where happiness was the main aim, where there was an atmosphere of love and security, and where life was always exciting, these children were amazingly confident, They had acquired an outstanding degree of self-discipline, they could be trusted to come into school early, and get on with some work of their own choice. They read everything they could lay their hands on, at their own level of development, they wrote very well, and talked very fluently, and they could discuss, reason and think for themselves.

I can remember talking with a group of rising sevens one day and Sandra saying 'Now then Miss –, speaking of mythology, let's take Neptune' – and so we 'took' Neptune, and every other god and goddess. We continued by discussing the theory of evolution, and ended with a long debate about what happened to us all when we died.

These children had a settled home background with families around them and they were put into an exciting, interesting, happy and secure environment in school. They were given the opportunity to work at their own speed, they were supported by an abundance of praise and encouragement, and almost all of them had the support and backing of their parents.

But for the last two years I have been working in a mining community on a new Coal Board estate, where everything is vastly different even though it is only four miles away from the one I left.

Our new school is in the centre of a new estate of almost 2,000 houses on the edge of the town, and quite separate from it in every way. There are rows upon rows of houses, two-, three- and four-bedroomed houses; centrally heated and with high rentals. Each house has a small back garden, but the fronts are open plan and cared for by the Council, and no ball games are allowed on the grassed areas.

Until the new working-men's club was opened quite

recently, there was no community centre at all, and there is no church. The pub, the betting-shop and the fish and chip shop were built, in that order, and were followed by a small square of shops.

If you came up on to the estate and looked at the new houses, the new infant school, the new junior school, and the new high school, you might possibly say, 'How fortunate these children must be; what more can they need?' I can tell you what they need, but first I must tell you about the people who live on the estate because only then can you really understand their problems.

The estate was built to house, in the main, men coming to work at a new large colliery in the area. So we have a largely 'immigrant' population from the north – from Scotland, Northumberland and Durham. These groups do not yet mix easily, and are not readily accepted by the minority Yorkshire group.

The whole estate is restless and unsettled, and always changing. The fathers have settled reasonably well, they get out to their place of work and have a better chance of making friends than their wives do. A large proportion of the mothers are homesick, and do not like living here. They miss their families – they cannot pop round the corner and discuss a simple problem with their mums, and there is no one to baby-sit so they are house-bound day after day, and return 'home' as often as possible.

An unsettled mother is bound to create an unsettled atmosphere for her children. Restlessness is easily passed on to children, and some of our children have moved already several times before they come to school. Many of them move from, let us say, 'The Heart of Midlothian' on Friday and are brought to school on Monday morning knowing no one.

Can you imagine what it must be like to be five, to move away from everything which spells security, and within the space of two days be faced with a new town, a new house,

99

and new school and new teachers – where you do not know anyone?

The people on our estate have no roots yet, and they may take years to grow, because we have an ever-changing population; but we hope that the children will eventually settle and think of *this* place as 'home' – and they have the future in their hands.

As one might expect in a new community we have many overwhelming social problems. We have four times the national average birthrate, which means large families of young children – more young children than many of these young mothers can cope with, and there are no grandparents to help, so some of the mothers discard their responsibilities.

Because of the high birthrate the school was overcrowded almost from its opening day, and for three years running there has been no room for the Easter intake – 'no room in the inn' for children who desperately need to feel secure, to feel wanted, to learn to talk. We now have a strict zoning scheme in operation which while it may allow us to take in next Easter's intake, is not helping us in our efforts to get the support of parents. Happily this problem is temporary.

Most of our families seem to have come from areas where parents were not made welcome in school, and where they were only 'sent for' when their child had been very naughty, so they have a fear of school and of head teachers in particular. As they tend not to come into school they do not know what their children are doing, so some of them are highly suspicious of our methods. There are many barriers to be broken down here but we have made a beginning and are trying to persuade our more settled families to talk about school – to tell others that they are welcome to come and see us at all times, and by so doing we hope they will help each other to settle and make friends.

As teachers we would hope that the fortunate children would start school happily – able to communicate easily in speech with a fairly wide vocabulary – that they would know their nursery rhymes, have been read to and sung to – that they would be able to recognise colours. We would hope that they would have been taken out for walks and out shopping, have helped with the baking and dusting and that they would have been dealt with consistently in a secure and loving home.

Some of our children are fortunate in this way, but over sixty per cent are not. They start school already education-ally deprived in that they have difficulty in communicating in speech. They have pathetically poor vocabularies and far too large a percentage have speech defects. Added to this they have the extra complication of strong local accents. They sometimes have difficulty in understanding each other – and certainly in understanding us, just as we often have difficulty in understanding them.

Many of them are not talked to or listened to, read to or sung to, and some lack security to a frightening degree. Some have obviously never held a pencil – they cannot match red to red, or blue to blue. Many of them have no respect for their parents and as discipline can only come from mutual trust and respect they are difficult to control and have little or no self-discipline. How can they have respect for teachers if they have none for their parents?

But most seriously – they lack the backing and co-opera-tion of their parents.

Like all good schools, we take each child as he is and try to help him to make the best of himself. Most of our children start way behind, so they have much farther to go.

Our first care is not for the clever children who forge ahead, or for the middle group who are working happily at their own speed, but for the large number of emotionally disturbed children who make great demands upon us, who want attention at all costs – about the physically handicapped and the aggressive ones who are often facing greater prob-lems at home than many adults could cope with; and we are particularly concerned about the quiet, withdrawn children who make no demands upon us and who could so easily become more and more deprived.

Sometimes we feel that we are almost running a special school and that the only difference is that we have much larger classes, but we are determined that our children shall have as good a start to their school life as we can possibly give them.

What our children need most of all is TIME, and we are trying to see that there appears to be all the time in the world:

Time to be happy – to feel secure.

Time to talk – to us and to each other.

Time to play.

Time to create and time to destroy.

Time to listen, to discover, to experiment, and

Time just to stand and stare.

We, as teachers, are taking time to watch our children, to listen to them and talk to them, remembering that we can learn more *from* them than we can ever teach them.

The frustrating thing is that we know that given the right conditions – small groups, more adults, more 'ears to hear' and voices to speak, we could help most of our children to conquer and overcome their many difficulties. Maybe, one day, this will happen.

'The dormitory suburb isn't without its problems'

'We call to minde the too much indulgency of some
Parents . . . not to mention their fond ambitions'
CHARLES HOOLE

LIKE other communities the dormitory suburb has its
share of human problems, although these may not be so
obvious. From the outside there appears to be a new neat and
regular orderliness, a conformity of styles of architecture,
of wall-less lawns, garages, a high standard of rich contemporary furnishings and to a casual observer all looks right with
the world. It is when much closer contacts are established
with parents and children the true conditions begin to show
and the problems of home and family relationships come to
light.

Often individual homes are small lonely islands in a sea
of houses. The problems are carefully hidden from neighbours at all costs. Often heavy financial commitments lead
to problems of relationship between husband and wife and
these in turn affect the lives of the children. There are
homes where a mother has been deserted and left with
young children. There are homes where father is away for
long periods, perhaps earning big money in an industrial
centre so that the financial commitments may be met. The
result is that these young mothers are lonely and in need of
adult company. This is a problem that Parent–Teacher
Associations could help to solve. These mothers cannot
attend the usual social functions or educational session in
the evening because of their young children, but they
could attend an afternoon 'sewing event' or social gathering
and this would be more enjoyable if some kind of playgroup
activity could be arranged for the children. This could be
a beginning.

THE CHANGING PRIMARY SCHOOL

In many homes both parents work to keep up 'standards'. There is nothing wrong with this but it means that parents have less time to talk to, to listen to and to play with their children. In other homes there is a clean, neat orderliness with not a thing out of place. Not only were the houses built by the same hand but they appear to have been furnished by the same hand and on looking through the large 'picture' windows I wonder where the family works and plays. Where are the bits and pieces of a hobby? Where are the books? Where can the children (and adults) mess about? Perhaps the order of priorities needs to be changed so that the real needs of children are considered – needs other than a large TV set and the latest fashionable clothing or toys.

This is where the school can help by trying to provide for those needs, by trying to provide a different atmosphere, by trying to provide an exciting place in which to work and play. We can surround the children with books of all kinds, we can arrange flowers and pictures and collections of things and we can give them an opportunity to make and listen to music.

Another problem of the dormitory suburb is that of the changing population. New children establish a happy relationship with their teacher and the other children and just settle down when they have to move on as 'dad' climbs a rung higher.

There are of course very many happy homes with happy parents and happy children. Many of our families say that they would hate to leave for life in a town or a small village. So many are enjoying the friendliness and the feeling of being a part of the community. (And I know the school has helped to create this.) Many families have bridged the gulf between the old and new inhabitants and are now playing useful parts in the community. They are happy to have their children grow up in such surroundings, experiencing some of the joys of both town and country.

The quality of life in a dormitory suburb, as in every

other community, depends upon the people living in it. Like every other community it has its problems and many of these problems affect the lives of the children and are, therefore, a direct challenge to the school within the community. The needs of each individual child must be our very deep concern.

What about teaching in a village school?

THERE were many aspects of life in a village school which were certainly never envisaged by me when I began to work in one. There are, for instance, cess pits. Our village like many others is not linked to main drainage. Cess pits are not emptied as a matter of course as perhaps a new Head from an urban area might suppose. When 'nearly full' one has to inform the R.D.C.

Investigations to find out whether the cess pit is 'nearly full' are fraught with perils. This Head makes her inspection armed with mapping-pole, gum-boots and clothes-peg, at twilight. If the sewer men arrived during the school day all doors and windows must remain tightly closed during the emptying operations lest obnoxious smells get inside. (This is also the case when the muck-spreading takes place on the fields which adjoin our school.)

In a village with a preponderance of old people there are few who can be called upon to work at school. We have no reserve list of dining-room helpers or cleaners as schools in urban areas have. It is true that our local office has a waiting list of ladies willing to do domestic work at schools, but no one seems prepared to travel out here. By the time anyone has paid the bus fare to come from the nearest urban area to put in an hour here, the payment received is hardly worth the effort and expenditure involved. So we depend upon the health and strength and goodwill of our part-time lady caretaker, an unmarried lady who is also a general factotum in the village. She 'chars' at three houses, helps at the village shop on two afternoons weekly, ices cakes for special occasions and cleans the church brass and the local telephone kiosk. We know her difficulties so we tend rather to put up with things, and do not grumble, when cleaning is not properly done in school because we know we are at her mercy and that we couldn't get a replacement easily. The building is difficult to clean in any case.

We are heated by three coke stoves and two open fires and apart from all the work involved in lighting and keeping them going they cause a lot of dirt and dust. Our wall displays quickly become grimy and need frequent replacements. We teachers dust our book-shelves and flat surfaces daily if we wish to keep things looking fresh. Furthermore some walls are damp and flake on to the floor continually.

During a recent hard winter our caretaker was away from her duties for a month due to illness. During the first week in snow and slush whilst we frantically tried to get hold of a substitute through the 'proper channels' we two teachers cleaned out and lit our fireplaces daily and even tried to keep them in by going up to school late in the evenings to bank up. This caused a certain amount of good-natured criticism from our husbands since they had to help and provide transport and fill coke hods and scuttles. 'Do you think Mr A. . . . (Head of the new comprehensive school, our nearest neighbour) is stoking his fire and lighting his boiler?' 'Get your coat on and come home!' was my husband's greeting when he caught me at my chores at the end of the school day. Of course all protests were to no avail. The husbands had to roll up their shirt-sleeves and get going. There was just no one else to do it.

The same sort of thing happens when our dear old dining-room helper is ill. We have to set to and wash up after dinner otherwise the dirty dishes would still be there the next day. We have stopped trying to get emergency assistance through the 'proper channels'. We prevail upon one of our children's mothers or fathers to help out and our caretaker or dining-room helper pay them from their own wages when the emergency is over. This all seems to work satisfactorily and saves a lot of trouble. In this same unofficial way we have coped with clearing away extra rubbish at various times. 'Our Bernard', an elder brother of a school pupil, comes with his tractor and takes things to the nearest tip. We buy him forty cigarettes out of school funds as we do when he comes to move heavy furniture for us. Two lady teachers and a frail part-time lady caretaker just have to get in this extra assistance at times as going through the 'proper channels' would take too long and become too involved.

Any unwary man coming up our school lane, from the postman or anyone else, is likely to be hauled into helping move or carry some heavy object.

Disposing of scrap from school meals was also a problem to be solved unofficially. No one thought it worth while to come and collect a small amount daily and pay for the privilege. We get a friend who keeps pigs to come here daily. He doesn't pay anything – we are only too glad that he comes – and if necessary we would pay him! Food scraps around our old building would cause rat trouble – the adjacent farms have quite a problem with this. As it is, we have field mice from time to time in our building and we have to borrow a cat for a night or two.

Surrounded as we are by trees, our eaves and gutters are continually full of leaves. Clearing these out is a constant drain on the finances of the West Riding County Council who fight a losing battle.

We have in our playground an ancient hornbeam and in

107

our front garden an ancient cherry tree – both protected by the Forestry Commission. One of our Autumn time activities is sweeping and raking leaves and having huge bonfires. The hornbeam bears catkins, leaves and fruits, which all fall in due season. The eaves become blocked frequently and during rain storms fountains of water drop upon the unwary at unexpected places.

Birds' nests too block up the eaves and gutters. Swallows nest annually inside the girls' and boys' toilets and there are droppings and feathers to sweep up.

We wouldn't be without our trees or birds but they bring their problems.

Tradition demands and receives certain things from us. We provide the entertainment at church garden parties and socials, putting on dancing displays and concerts. We read at church services and in fact take over the whole of some special services as on Mothering Sunday and at Christmas time when we provide a Nativity play in church. It is easier to do these things than not. Maypole dancing carries on naturally, the children seem to require no teaching since they watch each other from year to year and pick it up pleasurably and easily when their turn comes along.

A Rose Queen is chosen by the children annually and crowned by the 'Lady of the Manor'. It is a treat for them and all the village who come to see it take place on the school garden.

A Christmas party with tree and presents is given annually by the same 'Lady of the Manor' who provides the teas prepared and delivered by a local shop. We teachers shop for individual suitable gifts.

The teachers are members of the Parochial Church Council and have to be prepared to read lessons at church when requested and help decorate the church for special festivals, Easter and Harvest, and the Head plays the organ in the absence of the regular organist. The last Head has served as Secretary to the Parochial Church Council and

Secretary to the local Women's Institute for years. All these 'duties' have never been written down. We love it all and do it willingly and cheerfully.

Discipline troubles are not serious when we have welcomed children in as five-year-olds, settled them happily to school life, bathed their cut knees, developed their various skills and helped them over their successive stiles. The happiest situations develop from day to day – visitors inevitably comment upon our happy informal atmosphere. This I think is an inevitable feature of village school life.

We have no fears about keeping our children a further year as is suggested in local re-organisation unless it be that they are missing something that they might otherwise gain in a bigger community with more teachers to work with. We shall try to let each child develop at its own rate and up to its own capacities in its own interests.

There is a period of unsettlement for our children when they first leave us and some truancy at the secondary stage in the first weeks. This seems to iron itself out before the first year is over but it would help if the first-year teachers in the secondary schools could in some way get to know the background of our children better. It would help them to understand the terrific problems that our children meet when they leave our little two-teacher school, to attend a school with over ninety on the staff. The change-over is fraught with perils for all concerned.

We two teachers find it difficult to leave the school during school hours to attend conferences at other schools but we would welcome teachers from our receiving schools if they would care to spend a few afternoons with us.

Family grouping – mixed age-groups – the integrated day – non-streaming – these are nothing new to the village school. We have been carrying on with it all successfully for years. It is our life. Older children help young ones by just being in the same room; their example and capable work are ever present.

We are confident that young children are encouraged to tackle harder things than they would do in a single age-group, just by seeing older ones doing things with success. Older brothers and sisters can see their little brothers and sisters at work mastering the three R's and rejoicing with them as they progress. A young child sent in to read to the big room, brings happiness to us all.

We are lucky we know to have a rambling roomy building where painting and craft work can go on all day without having to be cleared away before other activities can take place. We can have practical mathematics going on in a corner or outside, reading to the teacher, painting, clay modelling, writing all going on side by side at one and the same time with groups interchanging all day.

We know our children so well that we can tell immediately whether they are working to capacity or not and whether they need help. We develop a family relationship with each child. This intimate knowledge can bring only good for the child and looks easy to the casual observer. Relationships which exist because of knowledge over a long period are not easily made by a student.

We have had students here on practice who have broken their hearts trying to do what we do. It looks so deceptively easy. We have come to the conclusion that short-term school practices are not for us. We have decided that we can best help students by accepting weaker ones to deal with very small groups. For example, if a young girl isn't too sure whether she wants to teach – we can give her say an hour daily with two or three children, in one of our house rooms, to deal with a chosen activity, so that she can begin to know what it is all about.

After all, successful teaching depends very largely on a happy relationship between the teacher and one child and we can provide this.

The local colliery has close links with the village. In the first place the land in which the first shaft was sunk belonged to the estate. The landowner received much profit before the days of nationalisation. There was free coal and delivery and sixpence for every ton mined. Early workers lived in the village and the school was extended to take in the sinkers and headgear erectors' children before the new colliery village sprang up. And the contacts remain. It is to the colliery we turn when we want such things as a new maypole replacement, copies of our medieval church key, seven pit lamps (for the seven dwarfs to carry in our current production of *Snow White*) and a trolley on which to move our piano out of doors. This benefits the whole village as we lend it out at spring-cleaning time.

Through the good will of the local manager who had a nephew at the school, the colliery has provided us with a mini-bus and driver for little local expeditions arranged to take place at our mutual convenience.

With the beauty of the countryside at the door environmental studies can include nature work of all kinds, trees, wild flowers, stream, woodlands, all are within very easy access. The farming year can be observed at first hand. We have a dairy, arable and sheep farms all very near and happy relationships with the farming families who invite us over their ground at all seasons to see the different activities. 'Bring the children to see the lambs – milking – sheepshearing – potato picking – harvesting' – 'I'm sending a lorry to take you to collect the daffodils' – 'I'm sending the tractor down tomorrow to collect you all so that the children can get a turnip for Hallowe'en' – We keep our Wellington boots at the ready.

In the early days the requisitioning of fundamental necessities caused me much heartache and some amusement. Ordering coal and coke in a 'chalet loader' became essential after I had had to help shovel a ton or two from a deposited heap outside a small aperture in the ancient coal place. I now rush out every time there is a coal delivery to see that 'trebles' are being delivered. Ordering 'doubles' or 'singles'

111

cause obstinate clinkers to form in the stoves and all coal and coke must be tipped by the said 'chalet loader' system.

During the first hard winter of my work in the village school I was forced continually to send some of the bigger boys out to refill the coke hods, one of which leaked a trail of dust. At requisition time I talked it over with my caretaker and we thought it reasonable to order nine new coke hods – three for each stove, to save scuttles being filled during the day with all the resultant hazards. Was it a reasonable request? We thought so. Coal hods were advertised in the current Supply Catalogue at 8s. 2d. each. At the same time I requested that the rotted flagpole be removed from the garden as I thought it might fall at any time and in any case the flag was full of moth holes and dated by the look of it back to the relief of Mafeking! Back came a curt answer from the office – nine coal hods – surely not necessary? Three were sent pending further explanations. As for the flagpole – all public buildings *must* have one and a flag ready to fly?

They, the local office, sent three workmen, who took two days to remove the old pole and insert a new free standing one, and we were provided with a nylon flag (£8). I wrote to the office saying that if in the winter time I had to spend my time filling coke hods and raising the flag I should have no time to teach.

Further letters passed between me and the office. Should I ask the nearby colliery to supply me with some aerial flight to deliver coke direct to each stove? *Eventually* nine coke hods were delivered! The new flag has been flown on all public occasions since delivery but not without a certain amount of hard thought.

Neither of the two teachers remembers with absolute certainty which way the flag goes up. *There is* a right way and a wrong way – they can never find a picture of the flag at the crucial moment! On the first memorable occasion when the flag was raised, a villager passed by – ex-sailor R.N., he came to tell us we were 'flying t' flag wrong way up'. We send for him now every time it is flown to be assured that all is well.

The requisition forms in my early days were a struggle. A request for a new wireless – the old one was a museum piece and required a good kick before it would start – was answered 'We'll send you a pair of clogs, but no wireless yet until the new financial year starts!'

Our relationships with parents from all types of homes are good. We achieve this by trying to be scrupulously fair in our dealings with the children in school. We know the home background of our children well and where we might cause offence we are especially careful. We accept each parent as we know him. We know when a parent from a bad home is obviously trying to present his best side to us. We accept him in friendship and welcome him and our common bond is the well-being of his child.

Thus when our worst mother, dangerously pregnant, came running into school one day while the class was occupied at various activities and I was hearing a few children read round my desk, she announced to all at the top of her voice, 'I've come to say good-bye ter 't kids.' (Three in my class.) 'Doctor says I've got ter get ter 't hospital, waters 'ave broke.' I ushered her children out quickly, and we all waved her off, and I carried on as if nothing unusual had happened.

When the same mother was having a long stay in hospital on another occasion we welcomed her phone calls to her children during school hours.

When she calls in to talk to us and lets out an occasional swear word, we try to courteously ignore it.

We welcome all visitors from the 'Lady of the Manor' to our most simple farm labourer. We find that they confide many worries and problems to us connected with things other than our immediate bond, the children. We fill in complicated legal forms and make urgent phone calls for people who are inarticulate or who find the public telephone box bewildering.

Here at school we often wish that we could provide a meals service for our village old age pensioners as we do for the children. There are no old folks' homes or meals on wheels service in the small village.

It grieves me to send surplus food out for scrap when I know a poor eighty-year-old two doors away would be glad of it.

Because our village is a rural community in beautiful countryside it does not follow that our children's homes are of the best. The well-worn question as to whether nature or nurture has the most effect upon a child's development has been answered for me here. I have had teaching experience in all kinds of school in the centre of Bradford, where there was not a blade of grass to be seen, a smoky factory area in Doncaster, and in colliery villages where slag heaps are a part of the common scene. But I have found no worse homes than the worst we have here. Fortunately we have our fair share of very good homes to balance the few grossly immoral homes, and homes where there is definite child neglect and ill-treatment. Our biggest successes come *not* in the eleven-plus selection successes or common entrance passes – we have had our share of those – but when we know we have given love and encouragement and success to children who do not receive it in any other place. We try to provide a rich and full environment within the school building and to lead all our children fully to enjoy the beauty of our own immediate surroundings.

We are in an old building and we have no space

There are many old schools in existence and at the present rate of replacement they will continue to exist for a long time. What do resourceful teachers do when they want to use new ways in spaces which are grievously confined? Two Heads were asked this question and their replies follow.

SCHOOL A

The building in which my staff and I work is over sixty years old and this is the newest building that I personally have ever worked in. My previous school, which was my first headship, was over a hundred years old and like many others of our profession I look with envy at the modern exciting primary schools which have been and are being built in the Riding and all over the country. These new buildings are imaginatively planned to give the maximum of teaching and storage areas and facilities to assist the teacher to meet the situations of modern primary work, in other words they are a 'purpose built' construction for modern teaching of young children.

However we, in common with many other teachers, work in a building of another era. It also was 'purpose built' but for the contemporary educational methods of the time of its construction – a time when children were expected to remain in their desks during their periods of instruction, a time when the materials and tools of learning were limited and extensive storage space unnecessary, a time when a class was taught as a unit, a time when three-dimensional work was probably limited to the visit to the woodwork room in their secondary years.

So what are teachers like ourselves to do in this situation where modern philosophy tells us that children should take as active a part as possible in their own learning and use a great variety of materials when in actual fact we are in a teaching space not designed for such methods? The answer is simple but by no means so simple to put into operation. If through our thinking and our observation of children learning we know that the 'modern' philosophy is right, then we must decide that it shall not be the building which determines our approach but the philosophies in which we believe. At the same time of course we need to make inspectors, divisional officers, managers and so forth aware of our difficulties and to obtain whatever improvements are possible for the benefit of staff and children.

No matter how spacious the building we have we shall always feel we could do with more room, and undoubtedly in old buildings this frustration can be acute. We have little space for the free movement of children in the classroom, little space for the multiplicity of materials and apparatus required, little space for models and forms of children's work and little space for the storage of bulky unfinished work.

But, however old the buildings may be there is no need for furniture inside them to be old. The new furniture, light in construction and more imaginatively designed, gives us more space and additional space can be created by taking away the rigid line formation in which our children sit. Desks skilfully grouped and arranged can create space where the teacher most needs it. Classrooms need to keep changing to meet the changing teaching patterns and it always interests me when I visit classrooms to see how the furniture is disposed. The grouping of desks is favoured by the cleaning staff who have on a number of occasions when classes have changed from formal rows remarked how much more room there is and consequently how much easier is their task.

The grouping of desks needs to be directly related to the tasks and activities the classes are pursuing, and the variety of work undertaken by the children will usually be freely chosen by them. But the choice they make will nevertheless have limits set to it by the teacher who must plan carefully for those activities which will demand a larger area and those which are possible within a confined space. This difference can occur even in such a subject as mathematics which may demand large pulleys or may be confined to ladders, counters, number sticks and the like. At other times the children may be working creatively on ideas arising from a visit or common experience. Some will be using bulky things like empty boxes and cartons; others will be working on materials which demand less space, such as paints and drawing materials. For the first group there will have to be room to store half-finished models and the numbers producing such models must therefore be related to the space available.

The classrooms in old buildings were constructed as rigid, formal, restricting, rectangles whereas the teaching spaces in new buildings have exciting, useful and accommodating recesses and bays in which groups of children can work in relative privacy and isolation. In the limited spaces of our old school we try to arrange our furniture to achieve a similar effect. We place our cupboards at right angles to the walls and produce interesting spaces by rearranging our pianos or book-cases or teachers' desks. In every classroom there should be at least one of these contrived spaces to be used as a library or reading corner and it should be as secluded as possible from the rest of the room and made attractive and inviting by book displays, flower arrangements and simple carpeting. Other creative areas can be useful for woodwork, clay modelling and painting and so on. In old classrooms there are few places in which to display children's work but the backs of old cupboards can often provide such a display area if they are covered with hessian or corrugated paper or mounting paper.

As education has changed since our building was erected, the amount and number of materials used in classrooms has

117

greatly increased. New apparatus is being brought into use to satisfy the requirements of the changed approach to primary mathematics and science. If we are vigorously to pursue modern methods then it is essential to accommodate these changes, but of course they increase the problem of storage space. Much of our answer to this must be found in good organization. Whether the materials are going into cupboards, into drawers or on to open surfaces they should be well organised so that the children know readily where to locate them and the whole school should pursue a continuous policy of tidiness and training in which the children take their full part. When a tool or piece of apparatus is not readily available and searching and rummaging has to be done to find it, creating more disorder, the amount of space is again diminished. We can assist our storage problems by serious consideration of the numbers of things to be kept in the classroom. If children are to be engaged in a variety of tasks then apart from essentials, like pencils and pens, there is no need to store bulky supplies for whole class use, and materials like powder-colour containers and the like can be reduced to cater for two or three groups only.

To follow a policy of modern education in an old building presents real difficulties but with organization and planning they can be, if not eliminated, very largely overcome. I have tried to describe briefly a few of the ways in which we try to do so. The better a teacher organises himself, his room, his furniture, his materials and apparatus the better equipped are both he and his children for tackling active learning.

SCHOOL B

IN our school the classes are arranged in order of age, the eldest children in Class 6 to the youngest in two parallel reception classes. In the summer term of 1969 we had 397 on roll in five junior classes and five infant classes. These were in classes of forty-two with the exception of the reception classes which had thirty-one and thirty respectively. Five of the classrooms were temporary and the six in the main block were all just under 400 sq ft. Obviously in such crowded conditions, in what was an old rather drab building, one of the first jobs I felt necessary was to make the school as attractive as possible.

The next step was to encourage teachers to suppress their squirrel-like hoarding habits, particularly as space was at a premium, and discard old, dirty and useless equipment. Even an impression of space helps, so all displays were kept below six feet which is in any case more appropriate for children.

We softened the hard lines of the rooms and gave them a more homely feeling by bringing in more plants and flowers and arranging them carefully and this even led to some of the staff attending flower-arranging classes.

Then the re-arranging of classroom furniture began. First of all, one teacher decided to 'spring clean' one Saturday morning and I remember a hilarious attempt at two-tier seating – which led to a motto which has stuck for a long time – 'If in doubt sling it out'.

We removed very old cupboards, especially in infant departments, followed by odd shelves, old hooks, screws and all six inch nails. We put paint and Fablon coverings on poor surfaces. We removed some cupboard doors so that children were able to help themselves more easily to material and equipment, and return them carefully after use. A few low shelves twenty inches high were fitted along the length of one wall. Cupboards were placed at an angle to the wall and this created more divided areas for display. We had water on tap in all but the portable classrooms.

Everything was made freely available in school. The stock room, for example, was always open. Large storage drawers were strategically positioned and re-stocked regularly. We arranged things so that not only desk-tops were available for the children to work on but low cupboard-tops also. These were the children's natural play surfaces and so large paintings spread to corridors and hall and woodwork bench in the cloakroom.

Parents became interested and a working group of 'dads' met regularly on Friday nights – 'Dads' night out' – and designed and made a dual-purpose Wendy House/Puppet Theatre which stored flat. They also made a trolley on castors for a TV set, another mobile 'kitchen' cooker and storage for all equipment, a work surface and a mobile record player cabinet which children could move safely and easily from room to room.

We had the school re-decorated and we refurnished the infant classrooms. Scattered temporary classrooms can soon become 'isolated' so their surroundings were improved by children's garden plots. The children in the scattered rooms come into the main building regularly for TV, reference books, cooking groups, P E, and to visit other classes – and the younger children went out regularly to see what was happening in the outside classrooms.

As we have plenty of outside space, groups and classes often work outdoors from the very beginning of their school life; only this week I overheard a class teacher talking to a group of students saying 'Of course we trust the children (five-year-olds) to do this work outside on their own. How else are they to develop self-discipline! Self-discipline is something we spent hours talking about in college – but I admit I would not then have believed possible what we now do as a matter of course.'

We could not have done as we did had relationships not been good. While the simple practical attempts to improve were going along, relationships between children and parents were changing. Talk became more relaxed, more purposeful and more honest. The fears of teachers that a lot of movement means interruptions, faded away as children became more absorbed in their work – as did the teachers.

Perhaps being closer together develops in us a little more tolerance and brings us closer to the children. Perhaps because we have no wide open spaces inside school we learn to move more carefully and cautiously.

5

SOME PRIMARY SCHOOL
PROBLEMS

They must get off to a flying start

Why take them on expeditions? Haven't they enough to do in
   school?

Surely with the really slow ones you have to slog at it.

What do we really mean by compensatory education?

Deprivation. How it shows and what can be done about it.

They must get off to a flying start

'He shall do his work playing and play working; he shall
seem idle and think he is in sport, when he is indeed
seriously and well employed'

CHARLES HOOLE

*It is of the utmost importance that the child going to school for
the first time should get off to a flying start. Most heads of infant and nursery schools are at pains to ensure that each child
should set his foot firmly on the first rung of the educational
ladder. Set out below are two statements by Heads of schools
set in different areas.*

*The Head who has written this first statement works in a fairly
new building set in a 'comfortable' area. The school has wide
corridors which are used as an extension to the classrooms. It is
normal practice for all doors to be open and for children, teachers
and indeed parents and visitors to move freely and easily
about the school.*

THE success of a child's first days in the infant school is established long before his name is officially entered in the admission register. It begins on the first occasion he sets foot in school, which for the majority of children is when he is brought along at around four years old to have his name entered on the waiting list. From this moment he is an 'unofficial' member of our school community – he is allocated to a classroom where he has friends or perhaps even an older brother or sister, and the mother is urged to bring her child into school for the occasional half-hour whenever she possibly can. Some mothers are still a little timid – remembering perhaps the unyielding rigidity of the primary school as they remember it – and so for a number of children, visiting school may consist almost exclusively of participation in our act of worship once or twice a week, with possibly a very infrequent visit to the classroom. Much depends on the class teacher concerned. Certain staff have a happy knack of making new, shy mothers feel really welcome and very much at home, and within these classrooms the potential 'new entrant' is absorbed very readily and is spending the occasional half-hour with his friends, long before he comes a legitimate member of the school community at the beginning of the term in which he becomes five years old. A child with older brothers and sisters in school is fortunate indeed. From his earliest days he has probably been attending morning worship, his mother will have established a happy relationship with at least one of the class teachers and he will have spent a fair proportion of time within a classroom. In fact almost from babyhood he has grown up accepting the school community as part of his life, so to be left for the occasional half-hour while mother slips away is bliss indeed.

There are snags of course – we are well aware of that. When the number of children in a class rises above forty, then those extra children visiting for that occasional half-hour could become more than even an experienced teacher could bear, let alone the young probationer within a year of leaving college. Yet it is working successfully even where the teachers are very new indeed. There is every probability that overcrowding in the classrooms may become a serious problem as more parents take advantage of the privilege of visiting. However, by making even more use of corridors, entrance hall, assembly hall and administrative accommodation, and going outdoors whenever the weather permits, I think this is a problem we can overcome. My staff and I are so certain of the 'rightness' of this informal approach that I know we shall resolve any accommodation problems satisfactorily, should they arise.

Far more serious and more difficult to cope with is the parent who, having entered the child's name on the waiting list, promptly forgets school exists and fails to make any effort to bridge the gap between home and school. In these cases a home visit a month or so before the child is officially due into school rouses a number of mothers into action, but there is still a nucleus of young children entering school each term whose visiting has been either limited or nil. Perhaps we shall never entirely eradicate the indifferent parent – though this is only a beginning and we hope in time to have an even greater impact on the community around school. Somehow it must be done, because where there is an easy, happy and trusting relationship between home and school – a result of frequent visiting – then there are no serious problems for the young child entering school, but rather the thrill of really 'belonging' and being able to remain in school for the whole morning.

'Morning School' for the beginner who is 'rising 5' is both accepted and welcomed by the majority of our parents. There is no hard and fast rule about the length of time a child attends 'morning only' before he reaches statutory school age – this depends entirely on the child concerned.

Some settle amazingly quickly and are anxious to return to school for the afternoon session within the first week, while others may take four or five weeks. The time factor is of no importance – what matters is the child and the relationships he is forming in this new situation. A child's happiness and success throughout his school life depends very largely on attitudes formed in these early days.

This second statement has been written by a Head who works in a Victorian building with a forbidding exterior and small classrooms and so arranged that access from one room to another is difficult. It looks out on to one of the most dramatic industrial scenes in South Yorkshire. Parents come less readily into this school and have sometimes to be enticed into it.

I BELIEVE that before starting school at five a child should know what the school looks like inside, see and experience the classroom situation, meet the class teacher and know exactly where to hang his coat.

To achieve this I collect the names and addresses of all children in the area who will be attending the school at some future date. I am then able to compile a list of the number of children who can be admitted each term.

About four weeks before the actual admission I send a letter to the parents.*

Having thus made contact I am always pleased to meet the child and his parents at any time of day and they are taken into the classroom to explore the large toys, the house corner, sand, water and so forth, and meet the teacher. At the beginning of each term I admit the children in small groups of six or so, over a period of two weeks and try as far as is possible to put friends or relatives together, or

* This letter is set out as an appendix to this section.

125

children from the same street together. The reason I do all this pre-school planning is because it matters a great deal whether a child is happy or sad, whether he likes school or is afraid. I believe it is wrong to plunge a child into a completely new situation, feeling perhaps lost and bewildered. After all, he has spent all his previous life in the very closest communication with one person – his mother – in surroundings so much smaller and intimate.

It is also my one big opportunity to try and establish a friendly contact with some of the parents who aren't always so interested in school or those who are perhaps over-anxious, possessive or fussy. I make them all feel welcome and accepted from the beginning.

At last the 'big' day is here. Mother and child arrive and from the first I want them to feel secure, happy and among friends. In the classroom waiting for them, is their class teacher with plenty of stimulating apparatus around the room to keep the parent's and the child's interest and to keep them occupied. As the child's power of concentration is so limited at this stage, there must be a sufficient variety of apparatus. Parents are able to stay with the child for as long as the child shows he needs them. Some children are quite happy and confident and soon settle down and within fifteen to twenty minutes parents leave the school. But some children are immature and unsure of themselves and will insist on doing what is familiar because they haven't the courage to try something new, and here the parents may have to stay a little longer. This is not always as easy as it sounds because some parents like to get away at the very earliest opportunity but we do try to persuade them to stay on until the child appears to be more settled and content.

Over the years I have found that the children who take a while to settle down are usually the children who also create an uproar at lunch-time. Many show great distress as they see some children going home at midday when they are being asked to have a meal at school, possibly the very first time they have had a meal away from the family table.

The distress can arise from so many factors – the fear of thinking perhaps the day will never end, the fear of getting some food they dislike intensely, the fear of not being able to manage the knives and forks, the fear of meeting yet another batch of strangers, the dinner ladies. This period can be the hardest trial for some children in the first few days and so wherever it is possible I appeal to the parents to take the children home for the midday meal until such time as the children have really adapted themselves to the way of school life and all it entails.

I should very much like to be able to say to parents of all pre-school children, 'As well as visiting the classroom before John starts school, bring him along and enjoy a school meal with us.'

During the first few days at school the children are taken for little walks in and around school to see other children at work and play and although this may be a little bewildering for some, it does help the children to realise they are part of a big family and that the reception room is not an isolated community. Some of the children may have older brothers or sisters in the other classrooms and occasionally it helps to let these older children have short spells in the reception room.

For the first few days the hall is kept completely free of activities by the rest of the school so that the two reception teachers can use this larger area of space at any time of day to allow the newcomers to expand in their movement, to play with the larger toys – bicycles, see-saws, trucks, trolleys, balls, and so on, or just to run and skip about.

Later on, when the other children begin to use the hall for movement or dance, we let the little ones watch if they wish, and this helps when we want them to strip for movement.

Most children are full of curiosity and want to know how things work. They show a lively interest in animals and we like to have some small animal in the room (mouse, hamster, rabbit, fish) as we find children tend to lose their shyness as they watch the animals.

At this stage very few of the children are able to work together or share their toys. Our first concern is to treat each child as an individual, to be interested in his needs, to notice how he reacts to what we put in his way, and to make time to listen to anything he may want to say. Many of our children have had little stimulus from home and their conversation and experience is limited and one of the first tasks of the teacher is to help these children to become absorbed in an activity. A sympathetic understanding in everything a child attempts to do goes a long way to establish confidence and self-assurance.

We like the children to take home all their first pictures in paint, pencil or crayon, but I always make a point of telling the parents beforehand that they must treat these pictures sincerely and show a genuine interest in them. I ask the parents to come right into school to collect the children at the end of the day so that the class teacher can pass on any information arising out of the day. Quite often a child will hang back because he wants his parent to see something special. We are getting more and more parents interested enough to want to know what goes on in the classroom. As the days go by we try to introduce a fresh activity, such as painting, baking, or clay modelling, so that there is always something to look forward to and keep the children absorbed. In addition to all the activities we naturally find time for stories, rhymes and jingles for singing or just for talking and getting to know one another. By providing our children with this kind of environment and actively engaging the co-operation of the parents, I sincerely believe we are laying the foundation to help the children face up to many of their future difficulties, both social and intellectual.

The vast majority of our children settle down fairly quickly and it is only occasionally that we have a child who takes a few weeks or even months to settle in. Usually we find that this child is disturbed because of home circumstances, or perhaps too much pressure is put on him by over-strict parents.

This is the letter to which the headmistress refers in her statement:

Dear Mr and Mrs Smith,

I shall be pleased to admit your child, John, into school on Monday,   January at 9 o'clock.

The enclosed picture is for John and he will find this picture on his pegs where he will hang his coat and towel and on other equipment.

Will you please provide John with a pair of pumps (elastic fronts) and a bag in which to put them.

John will be in Class 7 and his teacher will be Miss Jones.

If you would like John to stay at school for dinners the price is 1s 6d per day, 7s 6d per week. We really like to have all dinner money at the beginning of each week. Quite often it helps a child to settle down more easily if he can go home for dinner in the first week or so. I fully realise that this may not always be possible.

Will you try and bring John along to school before the end of this term so that he can meet Miss Jones and see the classroom. You are welcome to come in at any time in the next two weeks.

We hope John will be happy with us and that you will take a lively interest in all that goes on in school.

Yours sincerely,

It is interesting that a parent from a commutor area rather than a working class area found this letter a little too simple.

Why take them on expeditions? Haven't they enough to do in school?

'The young should learn natural history in the wood and field first'

EDWARD THRING

There is much to be said against taking young children on long expeditions, particularly if the purpose is ill-defined or the preparations inadequate. The following two accounts, however, show how valuable well-prepared outings can be, both as a stimulus to learning and as a help in creating the relationships in which effective learning takes place.

FOUR years ago several members of staff who, between them, have interests in fell-walking, ornithology, photography, wild flowers and sketching, decided to include children in their week-end excursions.

From this beginning has grown a school excursion which involves, each year, sixty or more children in walking in the Yorkshire and Derbyshire dales, the involvement of a parent who is a keen geologist, days spent in a Forestry Commission area with a forester, visits to an ornithologist to assist with the trapping, ringing and recording of birds, the keeping of weather records for the local authority and an annual week's Countryside Course during the Whitsuntide holiday.

A coach is hired for the fortnightly 'dales' expeditions and a nominal charge made, the balance of the cost being borne from funds raised at school-parent events. Walks are undertaken in the Malham area, including climbing the waterfall at Gordale Scar and visiting Bolton Abbey, Ilkley Moor, Dovedale, Edale, Lathkill Dale areas. Nature trails have been followed in Derbyshire. Local walks are undertaken – following the local river, a day out with our geologist in the locality of the school, and walks after school.

This excursion has become so much a part of school life that children are now well-equipped with sound walking footwear and clothing.

The Forestry Commission warden was approached and now at least one full school day is spent each spring in the company of a forester in a Forestry Commission area a few miles away. The forester is a true naturalist and a day spent in his company is most exciting. This contact has led to the provision of tree seeds and seedlings which have been raised in the school and then planted out in a seedling bed in the school grounds and this year the first saplings have been transferred from these beds to the school perimeter.

An article in the local paper led us to contact the leading local ornithologist and groups of children have been able to join him and assist in the identification, trapping, ringing and recording of birds.

Simple weather recordings were undertaken in school and a parent then constructed a screen and the recordings are now accepted by the local Public Health Inspector for his records.

An animal unit, constructed in the evenings by teachers, parents and children, contains bantams (eggs used for baking in infant classes), rabbits and guinea pigs. Children have maintained this unit every week-end and throughout every holiday without a break.

The annual Countryside Course is held for one week at Whitsuntide. The first course was held some years ago at Grinton Lodge Youth Hostel in Swaledale and was organised by the teachers of the school. This has now developed into an annual course held and tutored by school staff and their wives/husbands and the tutors of the British Young Naturalists' Association at one of the B.Y.N.A.'s Field Study Centres.

The course planned for this year, as last year, is to be held at Littlebeck near Robin Hood's Bay. The very active programme undertaken is a culmination of the involvement with the school environment and the week-end walking scheme. The week includes such activities as visits to a deciduous forest, coniferous forest, collection and identification of fossils, a day crossing moorland using map and compass, visits to tumuli, observation of badger setts, woodpeckers, a sea shore study, observation of sea birds, a study of the port of Whitby, trawlers, harbour and an abbey. The evenings are spent in writing up and illustrating log books from the field notebooks, talks and films about the following day's activities.

A study has also been made of the township in which the school is situated and this was recorded on slides and tape and later shown to parents and interested people from the village.

The children at this school are in mixed ability classes and these activities have had a great influence not only on the adventurous children but on the timid and less able ones, and particularly noticeable is their improved attitude and approach to challenges in other fields.

During the same period the children and parents, who are from artisan class homes, raised £7,000 by out-of-school efforts, always involving children, to provide an indoor heated learner swimming-pool and the building to house it.

Older children go to the local old people's home every Friday afternoon to do the personal shopping for the residents; they have also entertained them to tea in school, the staff collecting them in cars. This summer a series of evening drives are arranged, followed by tea in school and returning the old people to the home.

Kenneth was a boy from a good home, an only child and a source of worry to his mother. In spite of all her encouragement Kenneth was so shy he rarely left the house, a trip to the shops was beyond him and in front of other people he visibly shrank. To persuade him to join a party for a week at Newlands would have seemed an impossibility. However, Kenneth had a great interest in rocks and in minerals and the chance to further this interest and the enthusiasm of his class, carried him on to the coach and away to a holiday hostel.

Kenneth spent a most miserable and tense first evening but as time wore on one saw him soon absorbed in the friendly atmosphere. He more than survived the week and some time later mother came to school filled with joy and gratitude. Kenneth had come home bubbling over with excitement at his visit but what was more, he went shopping without a murmur and that very week-end had amazed everyone by asking if he could go with a friend to join the Museum Club in Leeds.

John came from a wealthy home and had a brother and two younger sisters. He had no friends and was a sad sight to see, always standing alone. His parents could make little contact with him and he was always sullen at home. At school he found other children difficult to get on with and his relationships with people were always strained. No one thought Newlands would appeal to John but it did and for some inexplicable reason he wanted to go.

Some time later it was a rather worried mother who came to see us with the question, 'Did something happen while you were away, was John in trouble?' We asked her why she was so worried. She then went on to relate to us what a changed character John had been. He was so polite and helpful at home and had brought another boy home, things he had never done, but he would say nothing about his week away. Mother and father took this as an indication that something had gone amiss during the week and his helpfulness was preparing for this to be revealed. In fact John had undergone a very personal experience through which he had found out a great deal about relationships, his own with mother and father and his own with his class too, and this had to some degree altered his attitudes and standards.

Joan ate only chips; it is true to say she ate chips three times a day and if chips were not on the menu she did not eat. Her home was very poor and Joan went to Newlands at the County's expense. During her first day she drank only water and ate only crisps. By the time she left Newlands she ate all that was put before her and never failed to have a second helping. Joan was virtually a non-reader and a non-writer but whilst at Newlands her joy in having conquered Causey Pike led to a request to sketch the mountain. She produced a quite remarkable sketch which to her immense joy the warden asked if he could hang on the hostel wall. On our return Joan painted with great enthusiasm about her visit. This was not all though, for through her new-found strength in paint and her interest in her Lakeland visit her reading and writing developed. To my dismay however, for her welcome home she had chips.

These three children, who all visited Newlands in 1968, found out a great deal, a great deal about themselves as people, a great deal about their own personal relationships in addition to some very practical geography. If anyone should ask me, 'Why take them?' my answer would lie in these three children and in many others who through the experience of living together came to know themselves and others better.

What are the experiences which can bring about a great change such as these in children? To my mind the value of living together with a group of teachers cannot be too highly stressed; living as a community for twenty-four hours a day and in this situation learning to accept each other, with faults as well as good points; the discipline of the community not being imposed from above but growing as our relation-ships grow and becoming evermore a self-discipline stem-ming from a desire to help and a respect of those we are living with. This is an experience which does not suddenly end at

4 p.m. but goes on evening, morning and even during the night when we adjust the noise we make to give others an opportunity to sleep. In this environment living so closely together the values to be found are immeasurable.

What of our own contact as teachers with this group of children? To the child it means there is on tap a constant source of information about his interests. Perhaps a child may have a particular interest that he wishes to pursue. In the classroom he relies on his own teacher and the books at his disposal. Here, with a group of adults, there is a far greater chance that one of these adults will in turn have a personal interest in the child's topic. We have therefore a larger pool of knowledge and greater stimuli available twenty-four hours a day for each child. Where else do we find such a teacher-child ratio?

So far little has been said of the value of the actual destination but this too plays its vital role. During their life at school the children become evermore aware of their own environment, growing outwards from the home. By the time they reach the age of ten, many of them are only too ready for the stimulating experience of completely new and challenging surroundings. As teachers we can be their guide in the exploration of this new challenge, encouraging and guiding and being keenly aware of all that excites them. We must be always realising that some will find new interests, new success that will bring strength and courage to the work they do in school.

There will of course be those who prod and probe to try and discourage us from our travels but I sincerely feel that the experience of Newlands can be and will be, for many children, a time when they grow beyond all our expectations. They develop a deeper understanding of home, of mother and father, of friends and of themselves. They grow to know much more about life, which is surely what we are concerned with in education. Through our talking together, exploring together, sharing excitements and learning to live in harmony together, we as teachers reap our greatest reward, we come away knowing our children better.

Surely with the really slow ones you have to slog at it

'... Be sure to have respect to the weakest and afford them the most help'

CHARLES HOOLE

The following statement was written by a Headmaster who was particularly successful in a mixed school of educationally subnormal children situated in an area which offered little educationally to the children it produced.

SLOGGING at it seldom works with the really slow learner. One has to find out why he is slow. Let me illustrate this by telling a story which may be dismissed by some as sentimental but is nevertheless true. It is about a boy who by reputation is a bad boy. He is difficult to teach, and even more difficult to control. But, then, there is little wonder in that. Both his paternal grandparents, grandfather and grandmother, had known the inside of prison. His father was delinquent from an early age, receiving much of his education in approved school and Borstal. The boy himself, was conceived, it is said, in an act of rape which resulted in criminal proceedings being taken. Father later married mother, but such marriages don't have the habit of lasting long, and this one was no exception. There was a separation. Then father was killed when he crashed the motor-cycle which he was riding at high speed through a town centre.

SOME PRIMARY SCHOOL PROBLEMS

The boy was taken into care by the Local Authority when he was five years old. In the children's home he became a difficult charge. By the time he was nine years old he had developed very aggressive traits which could be interpreted as psychopathic behaviour. He was recommended for in-patient treatment in a mental hospital, where he remained for two years without schooling. The happy coincidence of two factors, his satisfactory response to treatment and his mother's forming a stable relationship with another man enabled his discharge to be effected and he returned home to live with mother and stepfather. For the best part of a year he had a home and a family. But stepfather was an epileptic and during this period his illness took on a more active form. Mother became pregnant and was not well. The boy became unwanted. The situation deteriorated and he was placed once more in a children's home.

At the age of twelve years, school now finds him to be aggressive, attention seeking, destructive and virtually incapable of the act of learning.

During a recent school outing, the boy paused by a wishing well.

'What's a wishing well?' the boy asked the teacher.

'People throw pennies in and wish for what they want,' said the teacher.

'Such as what?' asked the boy.

'Oh, that depends,' said the teacher. 'Whatever it is that they want most of all in the world. That's what they wish for.'

Expecting a trite reply he continued,

'What do you want most in all the world, John?'

The boy replied, 'Somebody to love me.'

Of course, not all children with learning difficulties have the bizarre life history of this child. Nor have they been, to the same extent, the pawn of such an outrageous fate. But extreme cases often by the very drama of their impact, illuminate obscure truths.

All children who find the learning process difficult need stable, affectionate relationships with their teachers.

It may be that the learning difficulties themselves originated in acute anxieties, mental conflicts or deprivation during earlier childhood. On the other hand, it may be that genetically determined retardation and school failure itself is the cause of mental distress. Whichever condition is the progenitor is not important for the practical purposes of the teacher. Beneath the failure lies a hurt to be healed by true concern for the child, a quality which must find expression in thoughtful teaching as well as in good intentions and sentiment.

In any classroom full of backward children, there will be as many reasons for backwardness as there are children. Some may be the unintelligent children of unintelligent parents. Others may be handicapped by the circumstances in which they live. There are homes where every value displayed is at variance with the values of school, and where the pre-school experiences of the child have lacked the sort of stimuli required for proper conceptual development. Other children may have been neurologically damaged to a greater or lesser extent by birth difficulties, or by injury or disease in early childhood.

Whatever the cause, many of these children are likely to show a poor performance. Many will be poor verbalisers and as school values, above all other attainments, the skills of verbal reasoning and expression these children are likely to be regarded less highly than most and will have difficulty in meeting the school's normal demands and expectations.

Where can a teacher start with such a class of children? Shall he begin an even more determined frontal attack on the fortresses of illiteracy and innumeracy using the weapons of conventional remedial techniques? If he does, it is probable that his efforts will effect in the children a short-term improvement. But research has shown that often when the stimulus of any such powerfully applied external drive has been removed, regression occurs and, over a longer period of time, such children may be no different from children of similar ability who have never been intensively coached.

In fact the formal remedial teacher who sees his curative job too narrowly can be likened to a doctor trying to cure a man with a shortened leg by pulling on it. It may be best to emphasise all the things he can do well and so help him to keep his disability in proportion.

Likewise the child who has learning difficulties. Some day the physiological psychologist may be able to make good the missing neural connections which differentiate intelligent from unintelligent school performances. Until then, it would behove the remedial teacher to recognise the child's disability and thenceforth to regard his task as showing the child how to develop in an equable and harmonious manner, despite his poor verbal intelligence, using and emphasising the positive aspects of the child's being.

Many backward children have excellent bodies. Likewise they have practical abilities which are superior to their verbal abilities. Surely it is only sensible to try to use the endowments which they do possess in the matter of their education, rather than to emphasise their deficiencies. Their bodies they can use as perfect instruments of creative and expressive activity. Approached in this manner physical education transcends its generally accepted formal limits. The child can be involved through movement and his body in physical, emotional and social situations in dramatic and symbolic form. He will learn about life, not by reading and writing about it, but by enacting it.

Materials too can be used for the expression of ideas which never could be achieved by the backward child through the medium of the word.

Yet words are important, because words spoken, words written, words printed and words read are the stuff of literacy, and literacy along with numeracy, is generally used by society as criteria of acceptability. For this reason the child must to some degree aspire to a state of literacy before he leaves school to embark on life in a literate society. But not to approach the development of verbal skills obliquely is to invite ultimate failure. And not to engage the child's creative energies is to make a wasteland of his education.

And, of course, the attitude of the teacher will make a world of difference to a child's progress. If he falls into the hands of someone who regards him as a bad job of which the best has to be made, heaven help him for his teacher will be patronising and will lack humility and either condition rules him right out as a person fitted to work with children and particularly with children who have difficulties.

Adult expectations of children are, by and large, self-fulfilling, and, to children, adult attitudes are patently clear, whether these are overtly expressed or not. Let an adult, such as a teacher, who is a significant figure in a child's life, begin to think of his role as one where he makes the best of the material he has; let a school be organised around the implicit assumption that perhaps it has to make the best of a bad job, then very soon it will find itself doing just that.

A teacher's attitude to the needs of children must be a positive one. Perhaps the first and most important need that a teacher can meet is the child's need for affection and acceptance. Paradoxically, this is particularly true if the child does not readily merit the teacher's approval: if, for instance, he is slow or naughty. One of the greatest tragedies of British education, geared as it is to the production of certain sorts of conformity and achievement, is the fact that those children who most need to find a real relationship with the teacher are the ones who are least likely to do so: the difficult, the deviant, the slow to learn, the unattractive. In fact, our society seems to have a built-in system of acceptance and reward reserved for the achievers. Those who cannot fit this requirement are punished by being deprived of the very things a growing child most needs; success, praise, warmth, identity. The good teacher will know this to be a truth, and he will strive in his day-to-day dealings with his pupils to redress this balance of favour.

What do we really mean by compensatory education?

'School should be for the less fortunate children what home is for the more fortunate, a place where there is work but where there is also laughter, a place where there is law but where there is also grace, a place where there is justice but where there is also love.'

GEORGE SAMPSON

'TOMORROW we will finish the model, and then we'll do the play, and you can listen to us read', say the seven-year-olds, and on most afternoons, as the children leave the classroom at the end of the school day the teacher reassures them, 'Yes, we will do all those things tomorrow'; but on Fridays, she has to disappoint the children by saying, 'To-morrow we shall not be here, but on Monday you can continue with the model, and the play, and the new books.' The children look disappointed and grumble, 'We don't like Saturdays, Sundays and holidays; we wish we could come to school every day.' 'I like week-ends and holidays,' the teacher admits, then she asks, 'Why don't you like them?' Their answer comes quickly, 'Because there is nothing to do at home; all my friends are here, my Mum won't let me make a mess, there's nowhere to play.' Their complaints reveal that even very young children detect some difficulties in their home background; the teacher is aware of many more problems which arise in the homes of the children and are detrimental to the full development of the child and she endeavours, as far as possible, to counteract these influences without antagonising the parents, or lessening the child's respect for his own family. Some of the background difficulties are caused by the area in which the house is located, or by the age and type of housing available, some are the result of poverty, or inability to make the best use of the money that is available, some difficulties spring from desire for material possessions at the expense of time and patience, some from poor physical, mental and spiritual health.

The school, of which I write, is situated in one of Yorkshire's less attractive neighbourhoods. From the upstairs windows a large coal mine can be seen, and three other mines are so near that even the youngest children can walk to them. Because of the mines the air is sooty, and any new buildings acquire within three years the look of grey drabness that gives the streets a dull, gloomy aspect. The majority of the houses date from the period between 1880 and 1900; then, between 1903 and the First World War, many more streets and the school, were added. The township was extended to the south by a large council estate from 1920 to 1936. Since then there has been very little building, except for the development of some large shops along the main street, the addition of some bungalows for old people, a library, offices and clubs. Less than a dozen houses have been built in recent years. Heavy traffic on the roads adds to the noise, dust and dirt; the efforts of the local council to improve the appearance of the district by adding trees, or flower-beds, are frustrated by acts of wanton destruction, litter baskets are ignored – or any rubbish that has been deposited in them is wilfully strewn along the main highway. Windowless bus shelters have been devised for the area because the normal type was damaged as soon as it was erected.

SOME PRIMARY SCHOOL PROBLEMS

All the children in the locality, no matter how excellent their parents, have to endure this depressing landscape, there is nothing that the school can do to counteract the effects of soot deposits on the exterior of the buildings; but it can give a lead in teaching tidiness, care for public property, a love of beauty and determination to keep surroundings bright through indefatigable cleaning.

The school is fortunate to have a caretaker who cares. He sweeps the large playground every morning; but, if a westerly wind whirls litter from the street into the yard, he comes again and again with his broom. The children are encouraged to help him by putting wrappings from their sweets into one of the five litter baskets in the playground, they take a pride in having a tidy yard and compete for the privilege of taking a waste basket to pick up scraps of paper from corners. There is a small garden behind the school, and old sinks make plant troughs at the front. The children help to dig these, to keep them free from weeds, to plant seeds and blubs, to water the plants in summer, to gather little posies to decorate the classrooms. Here they wonder at the growth of bright marigolds from small dry seeds, they take pleasure in the texture of snapdragon petals, they are amazed that the scent of lilies or hyacinths reaches to the far corners of the yard, they admire the butterflies, ladybirds and caterpillars that they find amongst the plants. For the children from the old houses which have no gardens, the opportunity to tend plants is a fascinating new experience, those who have a garden at home have the chance to show how much they know about flowers and tools; occasionally a shy child, who has never been a leader in any of the schools indoor activities, surprises everyone by his knowledge of gardening; and his self-confidence grows when he finds that his playmates respect his opinions. (One five-year-old girl knew the names of all the rose varieties in the school garden and was disappointed that her own favourite was absent; by an amusing spoonerism she always referred to this rose as 'Brosephine Juice'.) All the children are shown how to use a magnifying glass to see the intricacies of tiny flowers and insects, and they discover that in the stones and mosses of waste patches of ground there are interesting patterns, colours and textures. Watching the changing shapes of the clouds, recording sun shadows, looking at cobwebs in the dew, or grasses bent with hoar frost, are pleasures that are available even in the dullest back street once a child's interest in these sources of beauty has been aroused.

The school has an unusually large playground in direct contrast to the tiny yards where most of the children have to play at home; to have so much space, at school, in which to run, jump, hide and enjoy group games is greatly appreciated, particularly as bats, balls, ropes and sand are always available. Because of heavy traffic, dangerous railway embankment and bridges, the recreation grounds are not available to the children who live in the centre of the township, consequently schooldays and the opportunity for unrestricted movement in the playgrounds are looked forward to.

But inside the school there is a lofty central hall, so that even on wet or wintry days there is still ample room for games and dancing. A good supply of light, portable equipment provides for balancing, climbing, pushing and pulling, jumping and crawling; all these activities are beneficial to the child's physical growth and development, but in small houses in an urban area the children have little chance to practise them all. At least twenty-five minutes daily are allocated to each class for the use of the hall for physical education.

In an industrial area the school buildings become just as much affected by soot, and acid in the air, as the neighbouring houses; indeed most of the houses are painted more frequently than the school but, though this sixty-six-year-old school has an uninviting exterior, most visitors who

enter the building for the first time exclaim with amaze-
ment, 'How bright and attractive it is inside!' Paintwork in
cheerful colours, gay paintings done by the children and
displayed on the walls and screens, quantities of well-
arranged flowers, gleaming brass door-handles and bells,
combine to make the school look pleasant and friendly. It
is of course true that if a stranger were to go into many of the
terraced houses or council houses nearby he would find the
interiors spotlessly clean, carpeted throughout, and furnished in modern style, and for the children who come from
such homes it is important that the school should have the
same high standard. But for the unfortunate ones whose
homes are dirty and whose only piece of real furniture is a
television set, the welcome comfort of a clean, warm, bright
school is even more important.

Most of the older houses in this district have now been
equipped with a hot water system, bathroom, and indoor
lavatory, the council tenants have had these amenities for
years, yet, although all the children are acquainted with
water sanitation they need training in its use and are often
most reluctant to flush the school's lavatories. Sometimes I
have wondered whether a notice forbidding them to touch
the handle or chain, would have the desired effect!

Usually, where older houses have been modernised,
bedroom and storage space has been sacrificed, and this
has limited the amount of playing space in the home, and
the number and type of playthings available to the children. Where rooms are furnished with expensive three-piece
suites there is usually only a small table, quite unsuitable
as a base for a structure built with large bricks, and, as the
table has no over-hanging cloth, the old 'hide-out' under
the table no longer exists. Painting, playing with plasticine, cutting out and sticking paper, were never suitable
occupations for the sitting-room, but the big, old kitchen
table was ideal for them and this has been superseded by a
small folding table on spindly metal legs, that fits between

the refrigerator and the sink unit, and does not provide a large, firm surface for children to work or play on.

In the larger houses the mother probably goes out to work in order to provide extra money; when she comes home she has already done a day's work and has yet to begin her housework; once she has done this she usually impresses on her family that she has no intention of repeating the tidying-up process, and any pastimes that are indulged in must be those without any litter or muddle. It is not surprising that passive television watching ensues, especially in homes without many books. For children from these tidy, fashionable homes, the opportunities the school provides for all manner of creative handwork are very important. But as mother's insistence on 'looking nice' extends from the house to the appearance of the child, it is prudent to equip him with voluminous protective overalls before he is allowed to paint, use clay, bake, or play with sand. Some children are so frightened of 'getting dirty' and of what will happen when mother sees them, that they may spend many weeks in school before they can be persuaded to try to paint, use pastels or water.

When one considers how much more frequently a housewife in South Yorkshire has to dust her furniture, wipe her paint work, wash her windows, curtains, loose covers and personal clothing, than her counterpart in the clean countryside does, it is not surprising that she is often reluctant to add to her burdens by allowing several young children to romp or do creative work in her house. For such children to come to school, to be able to play with many other children, to be encouraged to co-operate with them in making a large picture or a village of brick is a great joy.

The school may often have to make up to the child in speech what the home fails to provide. A child learns to speak by imitating the sounds made by the people in his home and immediate surroundings. If he has parents who talk with him frequently and regularly about a wide variety of topics, he comes to school at the age of five with an extensive vocabulary. If the conversations have been clearly spoken, correctly phrased, and grammatical, he probably already has a feeling for the kind of sentence structure that he will meet in printed books when he begins to read. Some entrants to the reception class converse very fluently; but there are others who only utter monosyllables in dialect, or who prefer to nod or shake their head. The fact that in some homes there is a continuous noise of pop-songs, or speech, from the wireless or television set does not seem to help a child to talk, which he must do if he is to learn. Busy parents, shift-work, the absence of parents from home because of the popularity of beer and bingo, the awed hush demanded by television viewers, are responsible for some of the inarticulateness of some of our children. Even the week-end rides in the family car, with the warning, 'Don't talk to me when I'm driving; be quiet, I want to work out this route', are not nearly such good opportunities for questions and answers as the old-fashioned Sunday walks were. Even when the car has arrived at the attractive destination, the driver needs a quiet rest to recover from the strain imposed by heavy traffic and tortuous roads.

Quite young children are often conscious of a distinction between the rough speech of home and the correct usage preferred in school. A five-year-old boy once admonished his three-year-old brother, who had just been brought to school, 'When tha's in theer tha doesn't say "tha", tha says "you" and taychers isn't missuses, thems "ladies".'

To encourage the child to converse rather than shout the teacher provides experiences that he will want to talk about. Having a peg with his name and special picture so that he can hang his coat in the proper place, having a box or a tray for his own possessions, stimulates many a child to chatter with his classmates; pictures and names are compared and contrasted. The classrooms have a variety of display; perhaps there is a colour table with a variety of

147

different objects all of the same shade; the uses of the objects can be described, some things may elicit the immediate shout of recognition, 'We've one just like that at home!' So another small link between home and school is formed, and talk begins to be easier for the shy child. The inquisitive child finds great satisfaction in the 'investigation table" with its magnets, screws, magnifying glass, old clock, horseshoe, kaleidoscope, torch and egg-timer. The questions that have to be asked and answered before the child has exhausted his interest in these objects help to extend the vocabulary and improve the formation of sentences.

Arrangements of flowers, grasses, twigs, shells, pebbles, and other natural materials, are another useful 'conversation starter', not only for the pupils but for parents and other people who come into the school. On a large screen in the hall and in the entrance as well as in the classrooms, the children's paintings, drawings, patterns and collages are put up for all to see and to discuss. Models made from clay or waste materials are on view on the window-sills and they call forth a great deal of comment. Each week there is a small exhibition in the hall; sometimes it is a collection of Victorian and Edwardian toys; sometimes it shows different kinds of bark and wood, with numerous things made from wood or it may be a display of building materials gathered together after a lesson spent in watching the builders at work on a neighbouring site. As the children have to pass through the central hall many times a day they go constantly to look at and to handle the exhibits, and they talk to each other about them.

Visits to see people working in shops, the post office, the dairy, the fire station and police station, the farm and allotments, are great conversational aids. Occasionally a milkman, or postman, or the caretaker comes into the school to talk about his work and the children ask questions.

Because there are no black-out curtains in school the projector can only be used in the Head-teacher's office;

the children come in comparatively small groups and sit on cushions on the floor to watch slides of school activities, animals, places in the vicinity and children of other lands. The snugness of the little room and the darkness have a wonderful effect on the shyest most inarticulate children. It also has the only window in the school through which the children can see without climbing on to furniture, and to spend a few minutes in the upstairs room looking out on to the street is always a stimulating experience. Perhaps it is because the little room is cramped and rather shabby that the children are very relaxed there.

Many of the children in this area suffer from emotional and behaviour problems as a result of unstable home life. The extreme youthfulness and immaturity of many parents (combined with the love of gambling and material comfort) and inadequate budgeting, lead to many of the calamities. Money needed for rent and groceries is recklessly spent on bingo and other forms of betting; after a time no more credit can be obtained from the local shops, the parents leave the house and go to their own parents or relatives, probably the man goes to one, the woman to another, usually within a ten-mile radius. Then the children have to adjust to living with different people and making fresh relationships in another school; it is unusual for the migrant family to remain as welcome guests for very long, and soon it is seeking new accommodation in another part of the district. One little boy had been in five different schools before he reached his sixth birthday. When a family moves about in this manner the children have to leave behind them their friends, their pets, and even toys. There is a great deal of callous neglect of cats and dogs; some children give harrowing accounts of the father's treatment of unwanted dogs and cats. At school the presence of a hamster or other small animals comforts children who have been deprived of their own pets, and many insecure, unhappy temporary members of the school have looked less defiant when they have been made responsible for the care of some small creature in the classroom. It helps children who move from school to school if the staff has one long-serving member, for she will probably have met some of the family on its previous wanderings and this provides a link between home and school. If the teacher can give one of these children a very small toy to keep, a small treasure to put in his pocket and hold in his hand in moments of bewilderment, it will help. Small children take great comfort from tiny, portable possessions, and a very little doll or teddy bear, wrapped in a shawl, consoles them when they find themselves in strange surroundings.

Too many children have good reason to fear that the mother will run away or the father suddenly disappear. Debt is probably responsible for most of the broken homes; but forced marriages in which the young couple is burdened with a child before a house has been obtained or furnished, tend to break up. Before the final break comes there has usually been a series of bitter quarrels, temporary estrangements and reconciliations. Fights involving other relatives who side with one or other party, are all too common and are witnessed by the children. It is small wonder that many children from such homes are terribly insecure and frightened. But the daily rhythm of the school programme with its alternation of quiet and exciting periods, the orderliness and cleanliness of the school, the flowers and pictures, the readiness of grown-ups to listen to conversations, the absence of shouting and quarrelling among school staff, eventually have a soothing effect on these children; they find school is a good place to be in; for they often arrive just after 8 a.m. and can scarcely be persuaded to leave at the end of the afternoon session.

Sometimes a child has to face disaster – when, for instance, a parent dies and a child is brought up by the surviving parent, or perhaps grandparents only, he seems to recover fairly well from the loss; but where the mother or father disappears for a period then reappears and disappears again, the child suffers permanently from a feeling of insecurity which manifests itself in many unpleasant ways. If the teacher can succeed in gaining the interest of such a child in some form of school activity (painting, modelling, sewing, reading or games), she can keep the child from brooding over the missing parent during school time, and perhaps direct the child's leisure towards the practise of this creative craft work or physical skill.

At school the children need teachers whom they can regard as trusted friends, in whom they can confide and from whom they can receive reassurance and comfort. Meals helpers, the non-teaching assistants, the clerical assistant and caretaker, all play a very useful part in listening to the children's accounts of their pleasures and problems. The children rely on the adults in school to help them to cope with all manner of minor problems; when the need arises to find a suitable box to contain a first tooth which has just fallen out; or find needle and thread to replace a button, or secure elastic; or advise on the choice of leaves to feed a pet caterpillar; or retrieve a coin that has rolled down a drain. As she renders these small services the teacher will be expected to listen to a long account of some episode that happened in school or at home. A friendly relationship with every member of the staff raises a child's self-esteem and makes up to some extent for the lack of attention and love that he receives in some homes. The school atmosphere should be one of caring; caring for each other, caring for the appearance of the building and surroundings, caring for equipment, caring for the little extra details of courtesy and good manners.

Some parents respond to this attitude. One unmarried teacher received a card on Mothering Sunday with a note inside explaining, 'My little boy insisted on sending this to you. After all, you are as good as a mother to him.' Happy relationships between pupils and staff usually lead to better understanding between parents and teachers. This is an important factor anywhere, but it is particularly desirable in a district where some resentment still lingers towards anyone who vaguely represents 'authority'. New teachers are almost always suspect at first, and there is a spate of complaints that they favour some children and neglect others; but when aggrieved parents are encouraged to meet the new teacher and to hear her teaching, or are asked to suggest where exactly they would place their son in the classroom to avoid a draught blowing on him, or a naughty, or neglected, or less clever, or more clever, child sitting by him, they begin to see the difficulties of the teacher. If parents can be shown work done by their child's classmates helps them to form a better judgement of his ability.

Children are quick to sense an atmosphere of tension between parents, and often become very quiet and withdrawn because they feel it is wiser to say nothing at all rather than speak and be blamed for adding to the trouble. At school these very quiet children appreciate quiet corners where they can enjoy pictures, books, puzzles, and play with dolls. Listening to music, or making music, seems to have a special appeal to them. For the unfortunate children who are not only aware of domestic friction but who see fights or hear a constant noisy stream of invective, the noisier forms of activity that are permitted in school are a healthy outlet. Banging large pieces of clay; hammering nails, digging the garden, pushing or pulling large toys, climbing and running may release the tension felt by the children, and the energy expended on the physical effort of these occupations means there is less likelihood of other playfellows becoming the target for blows.

There are some homes which give little example of honesty, truthfulness, or conscientious hard work to the children. A great deal is talked about 'rights' but 'obligation' is never mentioned, the privilege is sought, the responsibility that it entails is shunned. It is not unknown in the

district for a mother to be convicted of shoplifting and for
evidence to be brought that she was instructing very young
members of her family to assist her in stealing. Six-year-old
children have concealed small articles they have stolen inside
Wellington boots or in the sleeves of coats. The standard
of honesty that the school desires is completely alien to some
very young children. Dramatising possible situations ('Pre-
tend you have found a purse full of money in the street.
Choose some friends and act what you would do') leads to
conversation about the wisdom of having a name in possessions, the assistance the police give, the unhappiness felt
when something valuable is lost, and the relief when it is
restored. The majority of the class knows what is the correct
method of dealing with lost property, and knows too that
theft is anti-social. Whether this attitude of the majority has
much effect on the minority is doubtful; but the desire to
be liked and accepted may persuade the few dishonest
young children that in school it is wiser to conform. If the
teacher always endeavours to keep the promises she makes
to her class, if she admits that she does not know some
answers, if she accepts that her carelessness was the real
reason for the spilt paint or the untidy cupboard, she is
helping the members of her class to be honest. She must be
careful to show when someone is found to be dishonest that
though she disapproves of this behaviour she does not label
the perpetrator as 'bad' and ostracise him. Where full resti-
tution of stolen property is impossible some token of
amendment is often accepted by the wronged child. It is
very rare to meet children who are given too little pocket-
money or too few little luxuries; usually the neediest looking
child is the one who has most money to squander; (children
who have free meals are often given pence daily for choco-
late); but some serious, intelligent parents give their children an apple for playtime and no pocket-money at all.
The apple is excellent, it combats dental decay and contains
vitamins, but, as one little girl wailed, 'It is no good for

153

sharing, you get germs if you let people bite it, and I don't want to give all of it away.' If the teacher will cut the apple into quarters the problem is temporarily solved; if she suggests to the sensible parents that an occasional orange and a small amount of pocket-money might be allowed, temptation to pilfer or to be greedy may be prevented.

The stories, poems, songs and prayers used in the morning assembly play a great part in teaching the members of the school how to live happily together. Anthropology and history show that man has a need to worship, yet at the present time few homes in this locality provide any religious education for the children. Several families send the children to Sunday School at the Methodist Church, the Salvation Army Citadel or the high Anglican Church; but far fewer people go as a family to worship together in one of these churches. In order to strengthen what bonds there are between home, church and school, hymn-books of all the local denominations are used so that hymns or choruses learnt on Sunday are re-echoed on weekdays.

The day closes with another brief assembly in the hall; parents who come to fetch their children from school know that, if they wish, they too can come and join in this simple hymn and prayer. When the children write about the features of the school that please or displease them, they often tell of their enjoyment of this time.

Teachers who care for and respect every child, no matter what his home background; who seek and foster the talent that every child possesses, who have a sense of humour that not only survives in, but brightens up, dreary situations, who can listen sympathetically and give practical advice and friendship, who have a religious faith to sustain them in frustrating circumstances, can create a school in which a child develops happily. Happiness, progress, success, respect and friendship at school compensate for some of the problems of a poor home. The school can never replace the home, nor can it counteract all the ills caused by a thoroughly bad home, but it can strive to extend the benefits of a good home – clean, beautiful surroundings, a friendly cheerful atmosphere, interest, kindliness, humour and affection – to all its pupils.

Deprivation. How it shows and what can be done about it

'A great care must be had that those children that are slow witted and of a tender spirit, be not in any way discouraged'

CHARLES HOOLE

IN the area where I worked as a teacher in a junior mixed and infant school, there was a youth club which contained a high proportion of members who were on probation and which was specifically designed to meet their needs. It was felt that more could be done to help those children if they could be identified at an earlier age, and so I was released from my job and seconded to the club for an experimental period in order to see if it was possible to find children in need of help at an early age and then to alleviate their suffering in the hope that this would minimise their teenage difficulties, and so lessen the flow of children to the courts.

When I started this work I spent most of my time working at and from the club. This seemed to be the sensible thing to do for several reasons.

1. It gave me an opportunity for meeting the members on an informal footing without any shadow of authority falling between us. This enabled us to become friends, and consequently, they talked freely in front of me, felt able to confide in me, came to discuss their problems, and to ask for help

when necessary. These relationships gave me valuable insights into their difficulties, and into their ways of thinking, and into the reasons for their behaving in the way that they did.

2. It gave me an excuse for visiting their homes – the parents more readily accepted someone who turned up on their doorstep saying, 'I've come from the club, than a complete stranger who had no recognisable passport into their homes and lives. While visiting the homes, I came into contact with the younger brothers and sisters of primary school age and under, and I was able to introduce into the conversation the suggestion of our starting some sort of club or playgroup fcr the younger members of the family. In some cases, I succeeded in so arranging things that the actual voicing of the suggestion came from the parents themselves, which was excellent. During this period, the parents had time to get used to me, to trust me, and to adjust to new ideas, and so they were able to co-operate fully when the time came for the initiation of our new ventures.

3. I had time and opportunities for meeting the staffs of other welfare organisations, for building up good relationships with them, and for interesting them in the idea of our new project. I talked with Probation Officers, the Police, the Children's Department, the Education Welfare Officer, the Medical Health Officer, the Health Visitors, the Mental Health Officer, the Child Guidance Doctor, the Speech Therapist, and in every case I found interest and enthusiasm and willingness to co-operate. These contacts were very important as they were the people who came into contact with the most needy cases whom we must help in some way. Here again, time was needed to build up a certain amount of trust and respect. With the help of the Probation Officers and the Education Welfare Officer I was able to attend Juvenile Courts which brought me into contact with the families concerned. I was also able to visit boys from the club who were in remand homes and approved

schools. This was valuable in that I was able to keep in touch with the boys, and it gave me an insight into what they experienced which helped me in my work.

4. A number of the members of the club were of primary school age. By getting to know these boys I was able to appreciate more their needs out of school hours and I was able to use our acquaintanceship to advantage in school situations. When one of our members stopped to talk to me in a school corridor, it was not long before a group had formed and in this way it was possible to become acquainted in an informal situation which was preferable in this case to more formal approaches.

When talking with 'new' children too, it was a great help to be able to say, 'Oh! I know John Smith. He lives in your street doesn't he? Do you play with his sister?' Immediately, there was a link between us, and somehow we were no longer strangers. The parents of these boys were links with other parents as well, and they often introduced me to other mothers who happened to be about when I was visiting. A quarter of an hour's gossip at the garden gate was often the most informative part of the day, and in this way I was accepted naturally by the parents.

5. My time at the club enabled me to work in close collaboration with the County Youth Service and with the Further Education Service and I found this a tremendous advantage. Their constant support, encouragement and co-operation was invaluable.

These, then, were the main reasons why I spent my first months on the job working at the club. I felt it would have been unwise to rush headlong into the task I had been given. People need time to adjust to new ideas and to new people, and in the long run, I think this was time very well spent. I left the schools until the last as I thought I ought to prepare myself as fully as possible before approaching them. Once I had made firm contacts in as many organisations as possible, and had had experience with the children and with the parents, I turned to the schools. Here again, I thought it would be unwise to try to cover all the twelve primary schools in the town, and so I concentrated on the schools which served a large housing estate near the club. I chose this area because, at that time, most of the club members came from there, and so I had already established contacts with people who lived on the estate, and because in the previous three years, sixty-five boys and girls from that part of the town had been before the Courts. Therefore it seemed to me that something ought to be done about it as soon as possible.

I visited the three schools involved many times before I began any regular work there, so that the children and the staffs would get used to the idea of my being around, and so that we would get to know each other naturally. Most of my time was spent at the infant school because of the necessity to find the children in need of help at as early an age as possible. After preliminary discussions with the staff and with the Headmistress who had worked there for many years and who, consequently, knew the children and their backgrounds thoroughly, I began withdrawing specially selected children from their classes for half an hour each week. Because of all the foundations which had been laid, there were no problems involved in the withdrawing of the children. They were delighted to come with me and somewhat honoured that they had been chosen. The major difficulty was in having to refuse many of the other children who wanted to come too. We spent the time together talking, or reading stories, or playing games, or going for walks, or on other activities. What we did, however, was relatively unimportant. The important thing was that we were spending the time getting to know each other and building up relationships with each other. This contact continued when the children moved up into the junior school and was particularly beneficial to some of the more insecure children who found the transition difficult.

SOME PRIMARY SCHOOL PROBLEMS

The work in the other two schools was less intensive. One of these was the junior school to which the children from the infant school moved, and the other was a junior mixed and infant school which served part of the estate, but where most of the children came from 'better-class' homes. This school also took in the children from the local children's home who were badly in need of as much individual attention as they could get. In these schools I did not withdraw children from their classes (except for the children whom I had at the infant school, of course) and the contact was kept more informal quite deliberately because of the pressure of work which would build up in the years to come. The exception to this rule was a group of boys from the children's home whom I took home with me once a week because it seemed to me that a home situation would be of more value to them than anything that might happen in any sort of an institution.

From this work in schools it has been possible to determine fairly easily which are the children who are most likely to encounter difficulties later on and it would seem that, on this estate at least, approximately one fifth of the school population are in need of help of one kind or another.

The following list of symptoms of deprivation displayed in school by children of primary school age was compiled by teachers who come into daily contact with these children in the three schools I have mentioned and by several other teachers whom I know personally and who have had many years of experience in teaching similar children:

Demanding attention
Demanding affection
Demanding approval, even for routine work
Naughtiness
Whining
Uncleanliness
Poor clothes
Dirty clothes

159

Aggression

Backwardness

Poor speech

Stealing – if only to give away

Boasting – compensatory lying

Lying

Destructiveness – children at youngest level chew things

Hunger

Fraying clothing

Bad table manners

Fussiness

Unpunctuality

Truancy

Indifference – don't care about anything

Tale telling

Restless and fidgety

Inarticulate

Timid and withdrawn

Need physical contact

Sexually precocious – interfering, displaying, etc.

Very slow improvement in work

Deterioration in work

Erratic work from more intelligent children

No lasting effect from attention and/or correction

Bullying

Can't make friends and therefore tease – nipping, etc.

Cry easily

Parents who like to protect children

Nervous habits – nail-biting, thumb-sucking, twitching, etc.

Over-eager to please

Older children may avoid teacher (ten–eleven years old)

Sullen and moody

Don't like correction

Acquisitiveness – goods, food, etc.

Defiance

Sneaky and underhand

Hardness – unapproachable

Cruelty and viciousness

Lack of self-control

Dirty habits to get attention

Exaggerated reactions

Solitary – tends to be apart from current group

Lack of minor medical attention

Absence of parent-teacher collaboration

Petty, spiteful damage to other children's property

Exhibitionism

Unduly rebellious – will disrupt activities

Excessive indulgence in fantasies

Exaggerate

Agree to do things and never do – can't accept responsibility

Inability to make decisions

Retarded development

Inability to concentrate

Lack of interest

Inability to co-operate with others

Inability to communicate with others.

Recommendation – example, love and security from a respected adult with whom a relationship has been firmly established.

Characteristics which distinguished children they had known who had got into trouble with the police later on, from children who were deprived but not necessarily at risk, were sullenness, moodiness, backwardness, slyness, hardness, truancy, cruelty and viciousness.

This list is by no means exhaustive as it was only put together in the course of my contacts with the schools and teachers already mentioned and the symptoms are not listed in any sort of priority. It does show, however, how many are the ways in which children display their need for help and how many different forms deprivation can take.

It is possible to distinguish six main categories of deprivation.

1. Children Under Stress:
   Parents over-anxious
   Parents over-possessive
   Parents over-ambitious
   Parents who quarrel or even fight
   Parents who spoil their children and/or 'smother' them
   Parents who are jealous of their child's affection, interest, independence and development
   Parents who vie with each other for their child's affection
   Parents with conflicting views on their child's upbringing and future
   Parents who are anti-authority in any form
   Parents who are divorced or separated
   Children living with grandparents during the week and with parents at week-ends
   Children with a stepmother or a stepfather, especially if there are other children from that association
   Children who have a 'favourite' to compete with
   Children living with continual criticism or ridicule of themselves and their ideas
   Children who have to face a conflict between standards at home and standards at school or the standards of their friends
   Children who are conscious of being different from the others, particularly if they are not secure at home
   Elderly parents
   Domineering parents – one or both
2. Unwanted children:
   Illegitimate children
   Children resented by one or both parents
   Children blamed for circumstances, even for marriage
   Children with stepmother or stepfather

Children in whom no interest is shown

Children who appear to be too much trouble

Children without parental approval who therefore get no value of themselves as persons

Children who are never talked to or, perhaps worse, never listened to

Children whose parents are divorced or separated

Children from a family where one child is the favourite, specially if there are only two children

3. Children with a missing support:

One parent dead

One parent an invalid

One parent chronically ill

One parent ineffectual

Parents too lenient or indulgent

Parents divorced or separated

Parents in conflict

One parent hostile – or even both

Children who are unwanted or unloved or insecure

Children of unmarried mothers

Father working away from home

Children with one or both parents working at night

Father in prison

4. Children with physical defects:

Defective speech

Defective hearing

Defective sight – squint, glasses, etc.

Obvious facial deformities – hare-lip, scars, etc.

Deformities of arms or legs or body

Child who is too small, too tall, too fat, too thin, etc.

Child with bald patches, eczema, asthma, etc.

5. Poor Home conditions:

Poverty

Large family

Uncleanliness – bodily smells, impetigo, lice, etc.

Badly fed – undernourishment, boils, styes, listlessness etc.

Badly clothed – dirty clothes, torn clothes, unsuitable clothes

Unstimulating environment

House-proud parent – a house not a home

Children with no place to play or no opportunity to play

Lack of sleep – lethargy, irritability, aggression, etc.

6. Children at risk:

Other members of the family in trouble with the law

Close friends in trouble with the law

Children who are easily led

Children displaying obvious anti-social tendencies

Children attending Child Guidance Clinics

E.S.N. children

Children in care

As these categories show, children in need of help do not belong to any one stratum of society and some children belong to more than one category and sometimes, too, the causes overlap. It is important to remember that some of these causes do not in themselves denote deprivation. For example, a child who wears glasses is not necessarily deprived. But, to a child who comes from a very poor home, who is a member of a family of twelve, whose mother is separated from his father and has brought another man to live with them, who is shunned by other children because he is dirty and smelly, who is not able to achieve any sort of standard at school either in work or in games, the fact that he has a squint and is supposed to wear glasses may very well be an additional, unbearable burden which forces him to behave in all sorts of deviant ways. It is the additional irritant to an already insecure child that is important and noteworthy. A child needs to be very secure at home in order to cope with the cruelty of his contemporaries, and, indeed, of some adults he may meet, if he is unable to speak properly, or if he is not allowed to get dirty, or if his mother is referred to as Miss Brown, or if he is afraid to express an opinion, or if he is the only one not wearing long pants!

These categories consist of contributory factors which I have encountered in the children I have met in the district in which I worked. The more factors a child has to cope with, the more serious the effect it has upon him, but it would seem that the majority of these children have certain obvious needs. I would suggest that the supremely important need is for somebody with whom to identify in order to give a feeling of belonging, of importance, and of value, whom the children know will care about what they do or say, about what happens to them, about what they feel and think, and about their problems and difficulties, their joys and sorrows. Other common needs – not in any significant order – are as follows:

1. CONSISTENCY. These children need consistency in the person who works with them in the treatment shown towards them in order to counteract the uncertainty they find elsewhere, whether it be at home, at school, amongst their own age-group, amongst other adults, or within themselves.

2. CONTINUITY. They need continuity of relationship with the people involved. It often takes a long time for a timid, withdrawn child, or even a superficially extroverted child to accept and trust anyone, and therefore another apparent rejection could do more harm than good. They need continuity of care, of interest, of acceptance, etc., in order to come to terms with themselves and to develop self-respect.

3. AVAILABILITY. There must be someone there whom the children can turn to at any time. To be really effective, help must be immediate. This is an ideal, of course, but at least if the children know where to find someone during certain hours of the day, and know that that person will

listen and help, then it is a step in the right direction. I think it is much more effective if the child comes to the adult. This, for him, is a natural situation, whereas his being sent for and interviewed by someone else whether it be by the adult concerned, or by the Headteacher, or by the Child Guidance Doctor, is a more artificial situation and can contribute in some cases to making the child feel even more different from everyone else if it is continued for any length of time. This again is not always practicable, but I think it is worth working towards.

4. TRUST. These children need someone they can trust, who will accept them as they are and in whom they can confide without fear of ridicule or rejection or condemnation. It is important not to break any confidences which have been entrusted to you and it is important not to break any promises which have been made.

Conversely, it is important to trust the children. People tend to behave in the way they are expected to behave, and children respond to trust. They see themselves reflected in your attitude towards them. I think this is true for all children and it is extremely important for these children, especially those who are inclined towards unlawful activities.

5. ACCEPTANCE. Someone who will accept them as they are is vitally necessary. Because they are conscious of their own shortcomings, they will respond most readily to someone who will accept them, their homes, their families, their differences, their behaviour, their appearance, without comment, condescension, criticism, any change in attitude and even without pity. Only then can they be sure that they are being accepted as important individuals in their own right.

6. RESPECT. It is only when we identify ourselves with someone that we are prepared to accept their way of life and try to model ourselves accordingly. It seems to me that we identify with a person when respect and affection are

present, and therefore it would seem to be important to gain the respect of the children and to respect them in return. In many cases, this is something which has been lacking in their lives, but to have any effect at all it must be sincere. The children will then accept and adapt themselves to that person's attitudes, standards and opinions without realising that they are doing so. This would seem to me to be more effective than talk, punishment, 'do-gooding', or any other external measure even though these may be necessary from time to time.

7. CARING. This is not sentimentality. Some of these children have suffered from sentimentality and all its ensuing cruelties all their lives. It is necessary in some cases to show physical affection for children when deprivation shows itself in this way, but as well as this they need real care which guides, directs and develops the child to his fullest capacity – care which fulfils his needs, corrects when necessary, expects standards of behaviour in himself and towards other people and their property, but which always remains basically unchanged and constant and does not allow for any change in the overall attitudes and relationships between the people involved.

8. INDIVIDUAL ATTENTION. Unless the groups that any particular person may be dealing with are of a small enough number for the children to receive individual attention, I would think that the children would receive little, if any, benefit, and that it may indeed aggravate their problems. Here, once again they may find themselves lost in a crowd just as they may be at home, at school, and at play. This applies particularly to the child who is quiet and withdrawn and unsure of himself who will be overshadowed by his louder, more demanding companions.

9. UNDERSTANDING. Children often behave in certain ways because they are desperately unhappy, or frustrated, or unsure of themselves, or on the defensive, or angry because of previous happenings. They need someone who is

sensitive to them and able to understand without being told, even though they may not necessarily comment about it. There are many underlying reasons for a child's behaviour and attitude. It is necessary to know the child, to understand and to help. This is important, for children do not always say what they mean – often they are asking you to realise that it is in fact the opposite to what they are saying which is very necessary to them at that time, or true at that time.

10. SUCCESS. They need to be challenged, stretched, encouraged, cajoled, or have done to them or given to them whatever is necessary for them to gain a sense of personal achievement. A child who has been completely dominated at home and is apparently incapable of making decisions may gain his first taste of independence by being encouraged to choose for himself the colour of the paper on which he is going to paint.

There is, however, no formula. Each child is an individual with his or her own special needs which must be met. All need sensitive, caring adults to help them in their own way. These needs are applicable to the parents too and this is just as necessary for the sake of the children – happier parents will automatically give us happier children.

There would also seem to be certain practical needs which these children have in common. They need:

A place where they can relax away from the pressures of home and school.

A place where they can relieve their tensions.

A place where they can play out their worries, aggressions and fears.

A place where they can be physically active. This need is most apparent in Junior school children. Physical activity is a useful way to relieve tension and can be a most effective 'let-out' when there is trouble brewing.

A place where they can be quiet. This is a luxury which children from large families may rarely experience.

A place for experimenting and creating in their own way and at their own speed with help when necessary.

A place that is beautiful or contains beauty in some form or other. This is something which they have a right to and which is lacking in many cases.

A place where they are welcome and where they can find understanding people.

A place where they are accepted as important people in their own right.

A place which is informal, but where definite standards prevail – standards of behaviour towards each other, towards adults, towards other people's property, towards the building itself and towards the equipment, and towards other forms of authority.

A place where there will be opportunities for the development of the more confident children and help, guidance, examples, and encouragement for the slower or timid, withdrawn children.

A place where they will find opportunities for taking part in outdoor activities often lacking on a large housing estate or in a town – some children have never climbed a tree, or seen a stream, or picked blackberries or seen a goat.

A place where they can find someone who will talk with them and listen to them to whom they will listen. It is most important to provide opportunities for these children to talk.

A place where they will find some sort of stimulus and cultural background – pictures, flowers, plants, music, stories, poems, pleasant surroundings and interesting objects both inside and out.

A place where there is fun and laughter and happiness. Some children encounter only misery and gloom, complaints, quarrels, anger and irritability at home. Laughter is a necessary ingredient in their upbringing.

A place where they are free to come and go as they like, where there is an open-minded attitude prevailing.

A place where they can get individual attention when they need it.

A place which will provide them with an opportunity for going on outings. Some children have never been taken out as part of a family.

I am sure it is important for children of the kind I have been writing about to have a place of their own which some time during each day will give them a feeling of security and a sense of stability.

I would prefer that such a place were separate from their own school in order to make certain that there is no conflict of purpose or standards. I realise of course that the provision of such a place would rarely be possible and where it is not the next best thing would in my view be a room or two in their school.

6

WHAT CAN GO WRONG?

TO DAY in our educational jargon we speak of the difference between child-centred and subject-centred education and the Plowden Report of 1966 leaned heavily towards
the former. Over thirty years earlier the Hadow Report had
made the same point when it urged that education should
be thought of in terms of activity and experience rather
than of knowledge to be acquired and facts to be stored. Some
fifty years before that, and only a few years after the public
education service was first established, the Reverend Edward
Thring, then the Headmaster of Uppingham School, made
the same point in the distinction that he drew between the
lecturer and the teacher who he said 'represent opposite
poles in that there is an antagonism in principle between a
subject put forth attractively, where the master does the
work and the disciple listens and the problem of a dull mind
solved, and dormant faculties roused to efficient powers,
where the disciple does the work, and the disciple's mind
is the subject, and the teacher is a practitioner on mind.'

The lecturer's approach to teaching he believed led to too
great an emphasis on memorisation, textbook learning and
examinations, all of which he roundly condemned.

He had little use for the poor deluded 'honour-man' whose
one idea is knowledge and who walks into the school, 'like
an old farmer's wife into her poultry yard with her apron
full of peas, to be flung out indiscriminately and with a
cheerful consciousness of beneficent superiority, and picked
up or not, as may happen.' He goes on to say 'What becomes of the birds who will not be fed or, who cannot pick
up knowledge like peas?' He likened textbooks which he
called 'manuals' to the plague of frogs in Egypt and of

examinations he said, 'If any seriously believe that the dead hand of external power can successfully deal with the most delicate and progressive of works true education their armour is impenetrable by any words.'

But he would have the young to 'learn natural history in the woods and fields first', he would have every teacher endeavour to 'delight, interest and fascinate the child by judicially providing melodious sounds and splendid imagery', and he also said that 'You cannot drop what hand, foot, eye or brain have really done; it is part of yourself, belonging to hand, foot, eye or brain. But your book work is shadow work, a parrot-like struggle with words, mere sound that goes with sound. Alter this.'

There is no doubt that in most good primary schools today the teachers are likely to be firmly on the side of Plowden, Hadow and Thring for the reasons which Thring aduces and for many others besides. There is even less doubt about the standards which are being achieved by the newer ways. To anyone who has made careful observations over the last quarter of a century the advances are astonishing and beyond question.

Primary school children now work unsupervised as they rarely did 20 years ago and show an enterprise and initiative in planning their own work which is quite new. They are able from the earliest years to sustain an interest for far longer periods than used to be thought possible, and the quality of their expression in writing and when using a host of other materials is far beyond anything which was produced in the early years of our century of public education. It is also true that measurable standards have risen as has been revealed quite plainly in the two pamphlets published by HMSO in 1957 and in 1966 and entitled *Standards in Reading 1948–1956* and *Progress in Reading*. In fairness, however, we must admit that we do not know the extent to which this improvement can or cannot be attributed to newer methods.

WHAT CAN GO WRONG?

However, all the good that we can find in the newer ways should not blind us to the fact that in any three or in any 3,000 schools using them, one will be the worst and we should learn from its shortcomings. Some of these defects may singly be of little significance and are no doubt characteristic of any poor school however formally or informally conducted. But it may be worth while to list some of these shortcomings which may be found in all kinds of schools, and the following are set out at random:

Too ready an acceptance of low standards of work.

Too great a reliance on stars, shields and other 'school ironmonery' as incentives.

Inadequate contacts with parents, particularly with parents of weak or difficult pupils.

The Head who sees himself too much as an administrator or manager.

The use of a method or technique because it is fashionable.

Too many rules.

Aping of the secondary schools by houses, prefects, head boys, prize givings, leagues, supporters' clubs, and the like.

Litter; dead flowers in jam jars; work poorly labelled and poorly displayed or displays consisting only of 'the best' in the class.

Rigid streaming and the streaming of teachers so that the best teachers have the easiest job.

'I can't take the A stream from Miss X she's always had it'.

Too few teachers with convictions about why they are doing what they are doing.

Too much punishment and discipline by shouting.

Too much testing, examining and recording coupled with inadequate records of individual children's all round development.

Attempts to measure those aspects of work not susceptible to measurement.

Hours 9 to 4 and 'this is not my duty'.

I'll do it if they pay me for it.

Queuing up for admission to school and no children in school before 9 a.m.

Poor organisation of materials.

Too much teaching to eleven-plus syllabuses and tests.

Books in poor supply, poorly kept and poorly displayed.

Too many comprehension tests.

'Work books' which demand futile underlining and blank filling.

Too much copying from reference books.

A library too often locked.

Producing booklets which have obviously involved little genuine learning or study.

Indiscriminate use of radio and TV lessons.

Poor liaison with the infant and secondary schools.

Few flowers or living creatures in the schools.

Pets kept in squalid animal slums.

Too little laughter in the school.

Too much or too little noise.

Teachers who are insensitive to the quality of noise in a school.

The criticisms listed above may be insignificant in isolation but a number of them together may be seen as a warning sign in any school. But there are other signs which betray the school which is using modern methods without any understanding in depth of their true significance. In such a school one hears more of 'self-expression' than of the 'expression of ideas', and of 'creativity' regardless of whether what is being created is worthwhile. If the teacher does not realise that to teach thirty-five children as individuals and to meet their every need is an exacting task which needs much skill, sympathy, organising ability and above all understanding of the way children grow and develop, there will be failure and some of it serious, and the harm done can be almost as great as when the last five in the mental arithmetic test are made to come out every day to have their

174

inadequacy paraded. When a class seems happy but is totally lacking in purpose it is no answer for the teacher to say with a winning smile 'Ah, but we are doing a project' or 'All our work is open-ended', or worse still, as one teacher put it, 'We are a muck and muddle school but we are all happy'. In such schools when the work is lamentably undemanding the effect, as one visitor to such a school put it, is that of 'a wet play time all day'.

At the other extreme are the short cutters and the crammers and the stream-liners who seem to believe that good is automatically achieved if children can be made to learn more quickly. Such teachers will use programmes and ready-made kits as their predecessors used text books, and they fail to realise that the vicarious experiences will rarely exert the same force as the real thing. The kit is available and if the children in Hastings and Naseby have a kit which deals with the battle of Stamford Bridge then that is the battle they must 'do'. Such practices fail to meet the point made so forcibly in the Hadow Report on the primary school thirty years ago that 'the starting-point of the work of the primary school child should be the experience, the curiosity and the awakening powers and interests of the children themselves.'

When first-hand experience is effectively applied it leads to a study which will impose its own discipline, and the understanding of the teacher will ensure that the depth and scope of the study, matches the age and ability of the pupil. What is needed is material to exercise the mind of the child and an experience, something which he does or in which he plays an active part, is more likely to do this effectively than a book, a film, a kit or a programme. But whatever the 'method' there is always hope if the teacher can answer with conviction the question 'Why are you teaching what you are teaching in the way you are teaching to this particular child at his stage of development?'